Kelly
+
Beth

Huck
'18

HUCK FLYN

ROCKIN' NAM

It was "Woodstock" in Saigon

Rockin' Nam

Rockin' Nam

Printed in the United States of America
ISBN-13-9781482520125
ISBN-10-1482520125

Cover graphics by:
Trudy at BeverlyHills310, Inc.

Special thanks to:
Stephen Mackey

Rockin' Nam

Rockin' Nam

CONTENTS

Rockin' Nam

Rockin' Nam

ACKNOWLEDGMENTS

To my family and friends … I'm
grateful to all who have supported me,
and never gave up on me.

To all my GI brothers and sisters …
you rock!

&

To my dear friend,
the "Brooker," David Brooke…

To my sister, Marti!

To Monica & Marisa,

Rockin' Nam

PREFACE

As you will see and read in the chapters ahead, the story is a wild one. This author wishes to reach out to those soldiers who did not have such a great ride with their Vietnam experience.

Although some of my pals and I had quite the romp, we are still very sensitive to the fact that some came home mentally and physically impaired, and others didn't come home at all. To these people, we have the highest regard and the greatest respect. If not for you, perhaps groups like ours wouldn't have had such a good time. It's a fact … there is no greater fighting force in the world today than the United States Military—past and present … and every day, our soldiers continue to show it.

Rockin' Nam

Rockin' Nam

This is a true story

Here's the breakdown … this is a
truthful and accurate account of my
experience as a young soldier in the
Vietnam War… 1970-71.
It's as close as I can recall. In some
instances, I have changed the names
of certain individuals or other
aspects of this story — either to protect
anonymity or to help the story flow.
Otherwise, it is a genuine
recollection of the incredible experience
I had in S. Vietnam, as well as the
stories told to me by other GIs while on
tour. It is from the heart, my memory,
and my perspective alone.

Rockin' Nam

Rockin' Nam

For Doug and Stoney

Rockin' Nam

Rockin' Nam

For all Vets everywhere

Rockin' Nam

The wall

Rockin' Nam

Rockin' Nam

INTRO

As far back as he can remember, I've always been a rocker. And there was no doubt I was *still* a rocker as I got whisked away to Vietnam in the early 70's. This is an incredible story of a California hippie musician, drafted into the US Army, and ultimately gets orders to South Vietnam. In a matter of days, he gets a gig as lead singer and lead guitar player of a "rock band."

Part excitement, part fear, I landed at the 35th Engineer Battalion (Cam Ranh) in the fall of 1970, and apparently I was in the right place at the right time.

In less than a month, the band and I were out on the road, to *ROCK & ROLL* our fellow soldiers. In time, we'd play every major base in South Vietnam, even filmed by ABC News at China Beach in Da Nang. We travelled and toured for the entire year like we were a big-name band in the U.S. It was uncanny how we melted into the life style. We made friends wherever we went and heard war stories from many. The most important thing was that we brought joy and a little "normalcy" to our fellow G.I.s for san hour or two a day.

We began entertaining GIs everywhere, from Dong Ha in the North to Can Tho in the South … WE WERE BAD AND WE WERE NATION-WIDE!

The story goes…

Rockin' Nam

The '60s was an epic decade, culminating with the year 1969 and spilling over into 1970 and 1971. There was so much mayhem going on in the world it was hard to comprehend.

In August of '69, there were the Manson murders in Benedict Canyon. There was the "Woodstock Music & Art Fair" in upstate New York. Who could forget Apollo 11? Earlier that year, Led Zeppelin released their first album. Hurricane Camille killed 250 people in the Gulf, and the Beatles took the infamous walk across Abby Road—so much more ... Elvis began his come-back tour, De Gaulle stepped down, the first X-rated film, *Midnight Cowboy* wins the Oscar, Gaddafi takes power in Libya, Willie Mays hits his 600th homer, Lt. Calley is charged with murder, the Mets win the world series, Sesame Street debuts on TV, Richard Nixon took office, and the US draft lottery was implemented for the first time since WWII.

I was 18 and had just graduated from high school. Later, (in December), while in New Orleans with a band I'd met in Hollywood, I got a draft notice. I eventually got orders to Vietnam In just days, I was in Southeast Asia and had landed a job in a "rock" band. You can't make this shit up!

We quickly rehearsed and went out on tour. We were to entertain smaller companies out in the bush that were attached to the 35th Engineer Battalion out of Cam Ranh. These gigs had many highlights and lasted a while but in the end, they sadly ended. Not long afterwards, I managed to lie, scheme, and scam my way into an even bigger, nationwide rock tour out of Saigon.

Rockin' Nam

I travelled to the big city and thanks to an inside guy (who befriended me and pulled some strings), I got to travel the ENTIRE country! Top to bottom! ...From the North to the South and back again.

We were singing, jamming, performing and bonding with our fellow GIs along the way. Hard to believe this kind of a gig existed during a war *AND* right in the middle of the culture-changing Woodstock era!

If all this wasn't enough, we met Steve Bell of ABC News. He was the network's war correspondent who tracked us down and really took an interest. We were filmed at the officer's club at China Beach. He also dug us so much that he arranged for us to do a noon show for hundreds of hip Vietnamese teenage girls (who screamed after every song like the Beatles) and a couple days later ... a POW camp.

This story has everything: drugs, sex, music, thrills—you name it. Scary times too... like hearing "incoming" in the background while performing. There was romance too, like having an affair with my maid every morning or going after a popular "Donut Dolly." (Affectionate term for a Red Cross volunteer). However, our efforts were the big factor. We really shined at the shows and saw the fruits of our labor in their faces. The soldiers would constantly tell us,
"Thanks, we really dug it."..."You guys were great."

In the end, we did one last "Woodstock-like" concert, (on orders from General Abrahams through General Westmoreland). It was outdoors, and we were to entertain hundreds of sick soldiers ill from drug and alcohol abuse during their time in country. We felt bad for these guys and would do anything we could to help.

Rockin' Nam

This book constantly focuses on one incredible year of music in Vietnam—during the late '60s and early '70's. In the end, I had an epiphany. I finally "GOT IT." I come to realize *WHY* I was there, *WHAT* we meant to our fellow soldiers, and just *HOW* much they counted on us (the band and I) to keep their energy up, their hopes alive, and their sanity in check, if only for an hour a day.

After partying hard for months ... the sex, the drugs, the music, the mayhem, I finally got the message of what the hell I was doing there! And just in time to make sense of it all. I knew what I had to do. It was simple! My job was to "rock" the troops and to help them pass the time in this crazy place! I was ready... ready for the road ... ready for the challenge...
One story ... One year ... One band ...

"Rockin' Nam!"

Special Feature:

Trailer from the up-coming film "Rockin' Nam!"

is at:

www.huckflyn.net

Go to *the 'Rockin' Nam & more' page*

Rockin' Nam

70-'71

Rockin' Nam

THE BIG EASY
1.

In 1969, a pop singer came through the publishing office that I was working. He had a couple of songs he needed me to put music to. He was not only impressed with my writing and my singing, but of my guitar playing as well. He asked me if I wanted to join his band and travel back to New Orleans to do some gigs.

Uncle Bob was pissed; he felt betrayed. Here, he had rescued me from going "down the tubes," and gave me a great gig as a writer at a major publishing company in Hollywood, and how did I repay him? …with a quick exit on some musical lark, two thousand miles away.

Later, I would apologize, although I think we still both think about it today. I felt bad; I was a punk. We *did*, however, wind up hanging out years later. I remember him popping into a gig of mine, up in Mammoth Lakes, California, where my blues band and I were playing a gig. Bob seemed impressed.

So, there I was (before I was even 19), partying in the "Big Easy." We settled into a seedy, three-bedroom, cockroach-infested apartment on the corner of Canal and Jefferson Davis Parkway. As days went by, we'd rehearse a little bit, but I don't remember much more than that. The bar they had was very seedy. It was called The Cherry Circus. It smelled of failure and stale cigarette butts.

The first few days were awkward. I was trying to get acclimated to this new lifestyle. I cruised around the city and wandered into this great store, "Crescent City Music"—hundreds of instruments everywhere!

Rockin' Nam

We eventually met the owner of the store. He was cool. He was talking to some clean-cut guy in slacks and a plain white shirt. They were chatting about "who knows what" when we got there. My friend walked me over and introduced me to the owner, who in turn, introduced me to a straight-laced-looking guy standing with him. He extended his hand and,

"Hey, I'm Billy … Billy Gibbons…how are you?"

"Nice to meet you," I said (no idea who he was.)

The manager of the store chimed in, "Billy plays guitar also and is putting a new band together."

"Oh, cool," I said.

We chatted for a bit, but not a lot to say because … I'd only been in town a FEW DAYS! New Orleans had a distinct atmosphere to it, and a unique vibe. It smelled of so many different things at the same time … Creole food, coffee, magnolias, and what-not. Of course, I didn't have much to compare it to. I always liked to think I was hip and worldly, but in reality, I was just getting started. It was such a beautiful city, with the Pontchartrain providing a spectacular background against the brilliant cityscape of the French Quarter.

SIDENOTE: One interesting fact: New Orleans had more graveyards than I'd ever seen in my whole life. It seemed like there was one on every other block. All those vintage French statues and historic marble sculpture were both eerie and impressive, all at the same time. I made a habit of riding the little train around the city from time to time. It had certain quaintness to it and I hadn't experienced that vibe since I was a little boy in my hometown of Evanston, Illinois when the grandparents would take me to the Lincoln Park zoo.

Everyone finally got their stuff as we all said our "thank-yous and goodbyes." As we left the music store, I still had no idea who this guy was. He was cool, but I didn't realize just who I was talking to. Silly me, it turns out that just a few years later, this straight-laced guy, dressed in a pressed white shirt and finely-ironed Hagar slacks, would go on to form a little group called, "ZZ TOP!"

On the way back, we stopped for a munchie and I got properly introduced to the "the Big Easy" lifestyle by purchasing a huge shrimp *Po' Boy* sandwich, for about $1.25. Good start.

I headed back to the apartment. I had to get ready for the gig. I was a little burnt but I changed my strings and got ready to rock. I was looking forward to getting this gig off and running. It was Friday night, and we were set. However, I got there and I discovered the place was dark and nasty. It gave me the heebie-jeebies. It was an old bar full of the morbid stench of stale beer. Onstage, I tried to make it happen, but I got so bored and hyper, I started acting of out of character. I'd play these blues licks around the singer's Top 40 tunes. On my break, I started doing a few shots (drinks were free for the band). I never really drank; that's probably why I was never very popular in school. While everyone went out, drinking and partying, (doing keggers and getting laid), I'd be playing a gig, or sitting on a front lawn somewhere smoking a "doob" and chatting it up with my friends and band guys. Across the room, two women were sitting at the bar. They were cute. In my opinion, one was a little cuter than the other. They were just socializing after work. I'm going to make the assumption that they didn't come to hear the band.

Rockin' Nam

I guess I was trying to drown out the fact that I might have made a horrible mistake leaving a great songwriter job in Hollywood for this. I guess I was trying my best to bury some frustrations. On this particular night, the more bored I got, the more trouble I was.

An hour went by; I had a few more shots. As fate would have it, the two beauties at the bar were still there and getting cuter by the minute AND they were NURSES! I loved nurses! They were a little older, maybe 30-ish … (so I guess, to me, they'd be cougars by today's standards), and they were still in their uniforms. (I loved women in uniform, especially medical). Anyway, they were chatting away with each other at the bar, and by now, I was pretty lit. I thought I could do *anything* with *anyone*, (as alcohol will often do). I inched over to the bar. (Stumbled would be a better word.) I was trying doing my best John Wayne. What a crack-up. I zeroed in on Clara Barton. She seemed to be the hipper of the two…very attractive to say the least.

SIDENOTE: You have to wonder what gets into a guy's head when he thinks he can woo the "poodie" after just a few drinks. (Later in life, I'd run into this dichotomy from time to time).

I had a few words with her, but they were mostly trying to talk with themselves and pretty much ignoring me. I had another shot. It got crazier, more bizarre. I started fantasizing about being with her. What happened next was a little fuzzy but maybe the most hilarious thing and even quite strange. I managed to lean over (as if to whisper in her ear) and wound up trying to kiss her. Can you believe it? I didn't even know them!

Rockin' Nam

I TRIED TO KISS A STRANGE WOMAN … IN A STRANGE BAR … IN A STRANGE CITY!

The plan failed and failed miserably. I leaned in and stretched my body like a pretzel to try and kiss her. I was out of my mind…way too much alcohol. I leaned waaay over, and in a freakish maneuver, tried to plant one … right on her lips. I leaned over. (I wasn't fully aware of it back then, but drinking will often bring on ignorance and embarrassment). So you can probably guess what happened next.

I FELL OVER, RIGHT ON THE FLOOR! FLAT ON MY FACE! I DID A BELLY FLOP RIGHT THERE! IN THE BAR! IN FRONT OF EVERYONE!

And guess what? … Nobody saw it! They didn't see or hear a thing! The band didn't have a clue. … NOBODY DID! I picked myself up and sat back down like nothing happened. If it wasn't so pathetic, it would have been hilarious. I eventually went and got my things and staggered back to the apartment. If anyone would have ever caught sight of this, it would have been humiliating … mortifying.

The next week came and went and it didn't get any better, in fact, it got even worse (if that's possible). One night, after the gig, I went into the French Quarter to hang out. I stayed out all night, listening to rock and blues. It was great. I discovered that there were great musicians in the southern part of the United States. A lot of people in the Quarter would, for the most part, go see Jazz and Dixieland. However, what a lot of people didn't realize was that there was great rock and blues in other parts of the Quarter. These spots were mostly hidden, tucked in back streets and side alleys, off the beaten path. Places were packed where "20-something and 30-somethings" were digging music and the bands were jamming in little hole-in-the-walls on the side streets such as Royal or Dauphine.

Usually, there was a line outside & down the sidewalk. I was very inspired. I felt that I had just tapped into a more serious side of my career ... I was impressed. I'd never seen or heard this kind of stuff. I was about to get a glimpse of a brand new phase of my musical future. I didn't know it, but this is what I'd been looking for.
"THIS is 'the shit'! THIS is what I want to do!"

I started hanging out all night until about 6 a.m., and then I'd begin, (what would eventually become my ritual), walking over to "Morning Call coffee," and grabbing a cup of chicory coffee, and two powdered donuts. This little treat cost me a grand total of 34¢ back in 1969.

SIDENOTE: Somebody told me that *"**Morning Call**"* is still there to this day. I'd like to get back there one of these days. I loved their coffee! However, I'm sure the prices would be a little different. I have lots of thoughts about going back to New Orleans, but I'm sure it's not the same city as I was in a way back then.

After my great night, along with a trip to Morning Call, I slowly walked all the way back up Canal Street to that wretched apartment. I tried to spend as little time there as possible. I'd lay my head down and somehow get some sleep. This activity went on for a while.

A few weeks went by and the band and I really started to drift. They'd do their Top 40 songs, and I'd get bored and play more blues throughout the verses. This wasn't going to fly, and before I knew it, it was over. I started to think about what was up next for me. I'd never been in this position before.

Some guys and gals I met at the bar decided to go to Denny's. We were laughing and carrying on. I happened to look over my shoulder to the corner booth and saw this skinny, bleached-skin looking dude with long white hair and pink eyelashes. He was sitting with friends, and everyone knew who he was, but which brother was it? I'd seen both of them, and I thought they were great. I walked over.

"Johnny?" No answer.

"Edgar?" I guessed again.

"NO," the guy answered, and then they laughed.

"Yeah, it's Johnny," he finally admitted.

"Wow, we saw you a few months back."

"It was in June, at the Newport Pop Festival."

The one in Northridge, California … you were smokin'," I complimented.

"Well, thank-you," he said.

"Great job," I added. He smiled.

"My friends and I really love your records, thanks for coming out and jamming in our neck of the woods."

He smiled and I headed back to my table.

"Wow, Johnny Winter," (thinking I'd impress).

"Ya, he comes here all the time," they said.

Geez … talk about a buzz-kill. Here I was thinking it was so special that I saw one of the winter brothers, an artist that just rocked S. California. (In fact, it seemed like only yesterday, we saw him in California).

The guys at my table were passing it off like it was nothing. I wasn't a groupie or anything, but hey! I thought it was cool that he was there. I guess the others had just seen him way too much around town. They were apathetic.

Toward the end of November, 1969, they'd had enough…they fired me. Bummer. I wound up calling home. My mother proceeded to tell me that there was a letter for me from the U.S. army.

"Oh, there's a letter here for you."

"Really…what is it? "I asked.

"I'm not really sure, but …"

"Well who is it from? (There was a brief silence). Then she said, "The Department of Defense."

"WHAT?" OPEN IT! WHAT DOES IT SAY?"

"It's from the US Army … It's about the draft."

"WHAT! WHAT IS IT?"

"Hold on … it says your draft lottery number is ….. Fifteen!" "SHIT!" I screamed.

I hung up, and a cold, hard, chill went through me. I felt faint. I couldn't quite believe it. What the hell was I going to do now?

"Wow!" I gasped.

I was feeling panicky. "Nothing like a little low-draft army lottery number from the Defense Department to sober you up.

I now had some decisions to make!

ANXIETY ATTACK
2.

AUTUMN - 1970

We were cherries! (new in country). We were flying into South Vietnam from Fort Lewis, Washington. It was late 1970. The Flying Tiger 707 airline we were on was about to land at Cam Ranh Bay, where we'd begin a one-year tour of duty in the US Army overseas. There was a buzz in the cabin of the plane. A lot of guys were talking at the same time - a lot of hysteria. There was a whole lot of yakking going on, and a lot of speculation about our fate in this foreign land.

As we touched down, many were trying to hide their fear. The cabin was full of nervousness, fake laughter, and paranoia. They were carrying on a "gab-fest" that would make even the *Vagina Monologues* sound bland. The scuttlebutt eventually gave way to conjecture as one of the soldiers spoke up (á la Rick Danko from the "The Band's" *Crazy Chester* verse or Crispin Glover in any film): shakily…

"Hey man, I heard it's so crazy over here, that when you get off the plane, they throw you an M-16, and you run like hell because of all the shit going down."

There were murmurs of agreement as my friend, Woody, and I just chuckled. We were nervous too, but we hid it pretty good. We had heard a lot of talk and jive about this place but, for the most part, we tried to ignore it. In my anxiety, I wound up spilling it all to Woody … my whole life story. I just couldn't shut up.

I was bragging on how I started playing music early, what bands I'd seen, places I played, girls I dated … just about everything under the sun. We had a lot of time to chat. I ran on and on … how I got into the army (Fort Polk, Louisiana, after the low draft lottery)…How I worked in Hollywood—that I recorded a demo at fourteen…How I was the first GI allowed to bring a guitar to basic training (because I could pick a little country music), everything. I told him how I played in a band in "basic training" every weekend with a soul singer named Reggie and a Cherokee Indian named Robert. I also mentioned that I spent time doing a "soldier show" out of Atlanta (Fort McPherson where we toured bases and colleges in the Southeast. We did a musical revue called, *Gettin' It Together*") but now— we're headed for The Nam."

Woody was impressed! He was from San Diego and could hardly get a word in edgewise. In fact, he was speechless. He quickly became my biggest fan and now decided to speak up—

"Hey everybody, guess what we got right here?"

"SHHHH … Wood-man. Damn!" I moaned.

"We got a real live rock 'n' roller right here!"(big cheer), he continued."

Oh man," I moaned. (I was honored, but I wished he wasn't doing this.)

He went on to explain that I played guitar, and that I'd played lots of clubs like the Whiskey and the Trip (No! I said I went to those clubs!). He continued …

"He's from LA and has been working and circulating with lots of celebrities from the music business including friends of some famous people."

He went on…

"Names like, Phil Spector, Frank Zappa, and Sonny Bono," Woody yelled. "And he's coming over here to party with us!" (big roar).

I did my best to try to quell this, but to no avail. Of course, there were the usual skeptics:

"Well you're here in the 'Nam, now!"

And other detractors—

"Yeah, you're not in Kansas anymore!"

Most of the chatter focused on the question of whether there'd be any action when we landed. The answer would come soon. The wheels squealed down on the tarmac, and the 707 came to a halt. The doors opened and WHOA!

All I could think about was that scene in *The Wizard of Oz* when Dorothy opened the door after it came down (where she became wide-eyed walking outside). The first thing I saw was a beautiful, blue ocean, as well as beautiful women in bright silk and satin outfits. They were brilliant and beautiful.

The sun glistened down on the water like King Midas was wading in it. The air had a quality to it …I couldn't put my finger on it, but it was different. We disembarked.

We all slowly walked toward this flimsy, funky, shabby, man-made hut where we were to check in after landing. The Sergeant and the other Ems were waiting for us … and they weren't smiling. I took one last look toward the road. I stared at the locals. I was amazed that some had baskets on their heads. Others were youngsters and teenagers, following along, smiling, singing, and skipping all the way down the road.

We got to the "snack shack and I pulled out some documents. I thought it would help me get somewhere.

"What are these?" A sergeant asked as grouchy as he could.

"Well, they are my letters of recommendations ... some professionals I worked for and a few things I've done lately. I'm hoping to do some jamming over here and maybe contribute my talent to the war effort. I'm hoping to get attached to the right company, possibly be of good use," I answered nervously.

All the guys in the shack were trying to contain their laughter. They weren't ready for me. They were about to get their entertainment fix for the day. I stood by like a geek. The dude in charge started ranting—

"Hey, Elvis, this is the 'NAM! Got that? (He raised his voice)." "Listen up! You get an M-16, some K-rations, a poncho, some other things, and that's about it. There's no time for nothin' else ... especially the horse shit you're trying to feed me right now! Got it? Now, I don't want to hear any more of your crap. I've got work to do, and you're holding up the line ... or do you want your buddies to stand in the heat all day?" he asked.

This guy was too much. He reminded me of some of the lifers I'd seen at a few of the bases back home. He just went off on me when he found out I didn't want to play "Army" and wanted to entertain troops instead.

"Well, maybe I'll get lucky," I murmured.

Woody chimed in—"Whoa, whoa ... hey, hey ... don't you know who this is?" I tried to wave him off, but he quickly stepped up.

"No, I don't!"

"I know who it is!" said the sergeant (a little tougher). "And I don't really care."

"Well, he's a big deal. He's a rocker ... from LA."

"Hey, he's played the Whiskey!"

The guy answers back,

"Hey, I don't care if he's played *all the alcohols*;

He's here now, and property of the US Army for the next year, maybe more," the sergeant growled.

I spoke up —

"Sir, I basically have one kind of skill and I was thinking, if the army could get me..."

"**SIR!?** SIR!?" he butted in... Do you see any bars on my lapel, Private?

"Sorry Sergeant, but could you direct me toward someone might get me into some kind of music thing? I had a nice run in the States and was hoping I could maybe entertain here and"— He cuts me off again. (Everyone in the shack has started singing in unison) -- *"Drea-eee-eeam ... dream, dream, dream (ala the Everly's hit)...."* (huge laughs). The rest of the staff was getting cocky too.

They had us over the barrel, and they knew it ... bastards! They were really fucking with us now. One of the guys chimed in, referring to Woody—

"Hey Sarge, maybe his boyfriend can sing too." (Chortling wildly and singing out of tune) —

"He ain't heavy, he's my brother." (exploding laughter).

Rockin' Nam

By now, they *all* started singing in unison—a bad rendition of the Hollies hit, cackling all the while. They were mocking us and enjoying every minute of it. I sheepishly walked away.

I strolled over to the next destination which was the posted area, the area where the bulletin board was located. We always had to check the board to see where we'd to spend the year. A lot of guys were sweatin' it. Soldiers were getting very nervous, and I was a little nervous myself. I was in a fog. It took me a while, but I finally realized that I was now caught up in a circus called 'Nam.

I had time to kill, so I wandered down through the complex in the sand, toward the water. I never imagined some of the shit I was about to see and never dreamed it could happen in this crazy place. One of the first of many highlights was this hilarious meet-up where I ran into these two freaks. They were a trip. It was down by the water and they came right for me. They looked right out of the Haight or something. It was apparent to me later that they were at the end of their tour and on their way home. They came toward me like I had a big old target on my back. I'm sure I looked like a "duck outta water." I was so green. Just like that, one asks,

"What's happening newbie? Just get in?"

"Where you from?" the other one asks (with a kind of Sam Elliott delivery).

"LA," I answer.

The first freak replies, "Lower Alabama?" (They howl).

"No," I said timidly. "Los Angeles."
They were sniffing something out of a plastic vial.

"Want some?" one of them asks.

They offered up some kind of whitish powder, but I was *not* ready for that!

"No thanks," I said.

"I'm getting ready to go to a mandatory orientation," I explained.

"Three o'clock, sharp?

"How did you know?" I asked.

"Man, we've been through this movie before!

"What do you do?" asked freak #1.

"I'm a musician," I answered. (They both almost choke with laughter).

"You're a musician from LA, and you don't want none of this? What kind of musician are you?

"I'm new, and trying to get off on the right foot."
"Well good luck, man," they said. "Enjoy the ride!"

"BYE BYE NEWBIE!" they yelled. Then they started singing that "Carpenters" tune, in unison—

"We've only just begun" ..." baahhhaaa "...

They both split, and they were as high as a kite — Laughing uncontrollably.

I was smiling as I walked away. These guys were a roll. They even LOOKED like they'd been through the mill. Little did I know, in a few months, I'D BE THEM!

Rockin' Nam

I headed back to the main complex for the mandatory orientation, 3 p.m. SHARP! As I got closer to the main area, I saw some recognizable faces but I was still in a fog, having just left the planet with those two freaks from the Twilight Zone Kind of like the character in *Beetle Juice,* when he stepped out of the house for a second and saw all those creatures while being sucked into the sand).

I got back and everyone was loitering around and nervously waiting with much anticipation. I remember seeing the urgency in their eyes. At one point, they were all checking the board at the same time. They all wanted to see where their reassignments would take them. It got more intense by the hour. Many were getting orders to pretty scary spots—places like Phu Bai, Quang Tri, and other crucial areas.

Finally the time had come: three o'clock *sharp* and our big orientation! No one dared be late to this one. It would have been a sure way to get on somebody's shit list right off the bat. That's the LAST thing I needed now...after what I've been through.

We all made our way to the gathering. The assembly was headed up by a staff sergeant, a lifer, and quite an entertainer. I don't know how the next scene could top the last one, but it did. A hilarious moment was about to unfold. It was to be a scene that I would still remember some 43 years later. it was the mandatory indoctrination. We all sat in anticipation and watched intently.

SHOWTIME!

Enter a big, fat, Black, caricature of a staff sergeant, named "Big Dick!" He was an army man thru and thru, A "Lifer" as we called him. He was robust, overweight and bellowing...this guy was unbelievable. He was about to give us an orientation we'd never forget. A Kodak moment for sure!

"Welcome to the 'Nam, cherries! My name is BIGGG DIICKK!"

We could hardly keep a straight face.

"This guy's a roll," one guy murmured.

He continued,

"OK, here's how it's going to be...You **WILL** do exactly what BIG DICK tells you to do. If you don't, you'll have to deal with BIG DICK, and BELIEVE ME, YOU DO NOT WANT 'BIG DICK' UP YOUR ASS! Is that understood?" he yelled.

"Yes, Sir!" we yelled back.

"SIR?" Are you sure you want to call me that? I ain't no 'Spit-shine Shake & Bake'."

"Don't call me SIR! I'm a sergeant. I earned these stripes!"

"Yes, Sergeant!" we scream at the top of our lungs. We could hardly contain ourselves. It was so hilarious that it was difficult to maintain.

He went on again

"Good ... now, when you find yourself wandering around idle, you WILL find something to do. You *WILL* police the area, pick up trash...and get all the cigarette butts! Do you understand me?"

"YES, SERGEANT!" We reply in unison.

"I can't hear you …."

"YES, SERGEANT BIG DICK!"

"Louder!" he yells … YES, BIG DICK!

"SAY IT AGAIN!"

"YES, BIG DICK!" we all yelled as loudly as we could. This went on for a while.

What a great intro to this place. First, the freaks, and now "Big Dick"—too funny!

"Tomorrow, you will all go over to Building 'C'. You will all go get a malaria shot. You WILL study the chow times. You will NOT fuck up. Is that understood?"

"YES, BIG DICK!" We howl again.

This was way too funny and shockingly hilarious…hard to maintain. All of a sudden, this big mountain of a man makes his way over to a dorky recruit and singles him out.

"Are you gettin' any of this, boy—that I'm BIG DICK, and I'm the law?"

"Oh, I'm all over it, Sergeant!" the kid yells.

-Eruption of hysterical laughter. Even the sergeant was trying not to grin. It took all our strength to not get busted or singled out. Silly, but it wasn't a scene we'll quickly forget. With everyone so tense and nervous, this orientation was great comic relief. We went to check the board again about their assignments. I was getting a little nervous ... nothing had posted for me yet.

SIDE NOTE: I never took a malaria shot. I had a gut feeling that I shouldn't put that kind of shit into my body. I had a premonition and I stuck with it. (For years, I'd become more convinced that I was right. To this day, I try to do the right thing. I've been that way ever since).

Another few days went by, and still I had no idea where I'd to wind up. I couldn't imagine shipping out to the bush where I'd have to deal with war! I was scared I'd wind up in a dire situation. I could wind up at the DMZ! I said some prayers and hoped for the best.

After staying up late, unbelievably, I finally dropped off to sleep. The next day, I woke up to the beauty of the bay once again. I swear it felt like a dream. It was hot and humid. In fact, it was hotter in the shade in 'Nam than it was outside in the middle of summer back home. I went to check the board and saw real fear in some guys' eyes.

I saw nothing with my name on it. I got nervous. I walked around for a while. A couple hours later I came back around and wasted some time. I heard some more music and was slowly losing patience.

"When I am going to get some orders?" I begged. I waited and waited. A couple days went by but finally it happened — At last! And it was good news as the verdict came down. I couldn't believe it! The orders were…that I was to stay right there at Cam Ranh! I was to report to the other side of the bay, to the 35th Engineer Battalion! …

"As a *clerk*? What!?"

Of all the places I could have gone, and I get to stay right here? Are you kidding me? All week long, I saw men crying as they read their destinations. I saw guys white as ghosts when they found out where they were off to. I almost felt guilty. I told few guys as possible. A little embarrassed, I slithered away.

We loaded into a big truck to the other side of the bay. I must have had a lot of angels on my shoulders looking out for me. I could feel it. On the way over, I noticed, once again, the scenery.

We drove past the beautiful local women, who walked along the side of the road in their satin-like brightly covered full length outfits. We cruised past banana trees, gorgeous terrain, and rain forests. It was fascinating. Here it was, eleven in the morning, and I'm riding along, and taking it all in.

I was thinking,

"Is this for real?"

All the families were walking together. There were all kinds of different crazy vehicles—it was bizarre.

When we finally arrived at the 35th, I thanked the driver, grabbed my duffle bag, and walked into CO's headquarters. I hustled up the steps to the Captain's headquarters office.

"I'm Flyn," I report.

"Welcome soldier, I'm Captain Jack, and you're now a part of the 35th Engineer Battalion."

(I'm thinking, "Captain Jack ... that's funny, kind of like the Who song."

"...Oh wait, that was 'Happy Jack' ... whatever)."

He started to explain my new role.

"First thing you need to know is that you're a clerk with the 35th engineer battalion out of Cam Ranh." You'll be making coffee every morning and typing during the day and various errands. You'll be working in the other room with everyone else ... Any questions?"

I took a peek into the other room. There were about twenty guys sitting in cubicles typing away.

"I'm a clerk?" I asked with a little sarcasm.

"Yeah, you got a problem with that?

"No...no, sir, no problem," I gulped.

"You're not going to be a handful for me, are you Flyn?

"No—no, Sir, I answered ... no, I'm cool, Cap."

The commanding officer didn't know WHAT to make of me and I decided to lighten up the conversation by asking,

"So, Cap, what's happening around here?"

"Well," he said, "the enemy has slowed the war down … ever since Tet of '68, the action has been at a minimum."

"Isn't that a good thing?" I asked. "I mean, doesn't that put everyone more at ease?"

"True, but now the guys are a little bored and getting lethargic so I've taken matters into my own hands and decided to put a band together—you know, to keep them loose, keep them entertained. I've got a bass player, a drummer, and I'm just trying to find a guitarist."

I couldn't even *begin* to believe what I was hearing! Quietly, I was thinking,

"ARE YOU SHITTIN' ME!? This is what I prayed for."

"I'm sorry, Cap," I said. "Maybe my hearing is a little messed up from the flight over or something, it was a long flight (I chuckled). I thought you said that you needed a guitar player for a band…isn't that crazy?"

I began to chuckle again, nervously.

"That's exactly what I said, Private!"

On the inside, I was pretty shaky. However, on the outside, I was trying my best to be cool. There was no way I was going to let this opportunity slip away—are you kidding me? The CO's putting a band together?

"OH MY GOD," I thought.

"Well, Cap, I don't know what to say. I guess today's your lucky day! I'm your guy! I've been playing gigs for quite a while now. I had my own band back home," I stated emphatically.

He wasn't that impressed. He probably thought I was just blowing smoke.

Let's just say, with what I told him, he wasn't ready to give me the Grammy quite yet — *OR THE GIG*! I was starting to worry that I'd blow this great opportunity and never get another! This is what he offered —

"Well son, maybe you can audition at the end of the week, soon as I get a couple more takers. I'm expecting some more transfers to come through."

"OH NO! No, no," I thought. "This was my big chance. I had prayed for this moment. I knew I HAD to have this gig!"

I decided to stack the deck, use a trump card, to dig up a really big LIE! I didn't want to, but in this case, it was vital.

I had no idea just *what* I was going to say, but, true to form, flying by the seat of my pants, I came up with a doozie … something from out of "left field."

"Sir, I'm sorry but I *have* to have this gig. I know that we just met, but I need to tell you something — I'm a singer, and a guitarist. I've been playing since I was 11, and … well … and … um … er …."

"Yes, Private? Speak up!"

"Well, er … you see … well, the thing is … um … well … I used to play with … ah … Grand Funk!" (DEAD SILENCE!)

Suddenly, everyone in the room got quiet (like the E.F. Hutton commercial). It was eerily still, and it kind of freaked me out. Everybody's staring at me, then him, then me. He looked down, pondered a minute, looked in the air, his eyes constantly searching. It was quiet for a few seconds and all of a sudden, to everyone's surprise, he raised his head and exclaimed,

"Really? I love that band! Garcia, go grab a 'geeetarr' out of the other room — it's in the rec closet."

While I was waiting, it was humid and uncomfortable. I reached up to free my arm from my sticky uniform sleeve, and didn't realize there was a ceiling fan directly above my head.

I pushed the arm up through the sleeve, and arched the elbow directly skyward, into the very center of the blades...I mean directly into the center of the huge, medium-turning, ceiling fan above. Unbelievably, I didn't feel a thing and I wasn't hurt. Imagine that! It could have been over before it even started!!!

"What songs can you play?" he asked.

"EVERYTHING, ALL OF 'EM," I boasted.

"Everything?" Cap questioned sarcastically.

"Well, most of 'em: Creedence, Hendrix, the Doors — try me."

The PFC. brought in an acoustic guitar (some old used beat-up thing). You could have heard a pin drop. It was strange seeing the guys all piled into the doorway. At home I was just another musician, (a dime a dozen) but here, I was special — different from the rest — unique.

All the years of jamming in the garage and listening to the hits on the radio had paid off. It's interesting, since I was on my own over here in 'Nam now, I acquired lots of confidence. And, now, spouting off about how hip I was. Besides, no one from the neighborhood was around to refute me.

I did a quick "tune job" and started in —

First, the G chord. BAM! Creedence

"Who'll Stop the Rain," followed by — BAM — Buddy Miles "Them Changes."

Rockin' Nam

And finally—BAM—the intro to…

"I'm Your Captain/Closer to Home" by Grand Funk Railroad …

"Everybody, listen to me…I'm your captain; I'm your captain … though I'm feelin' mighty sick …."

I finished to some applause and waited. I wanted it to happen. Dying to get this break, I waited for Cap to say it. He stood up and pondered for a sec. Then, he looked down. He looked away. Then with a big grin, and to everyone's shock, he finally came through … he said it—

"The band house is down that way. Do me a favor; go kick some ass!"

"YESSS!" I exclaimed.

I'm sure these guys were probably thinking,

"Where did this freak come from?" He just walks into the 'Nam and gets a gig in a touring rock band?"

They were shocked when the cap said I was "in." So was I—for that matter! "ARE YOU SHITTIN' ME?"

I made it down to the band hooch and met the other two. We bonded nicely. I guess that was the vibe in this era. I comically posed this question as I met my new friends,

"So, let me get this straight. We just show up at Cam Ranh, check in, audition in Cap's office, and a few days later, we're a band and on tour! How cool is that?"

"Isn't it great?" one of them said with a big smile.

I sarcastically thought,

"Boy, if those guys at the snack shop could see me now! They were so arrogant and pompous and treated me with such disregard and if this was just deserts."

46

Rockin' Nam

It was a great break, just what I wanted. I headed down the road ... toward the band hootch. To meet the new band!

We all got on nicely. We put a set together pretty quickly; we jammed every day and got ready to roll. I started my one-year duty in 'Nam with a bang and now this lucky break and timely opportunity to get to play music—in Nam of all place. All I could think about at that particular moment was the great adage- "Hell Yeah!"

Rockin' Nam

WELCOME TO THE JUNGLE

3.

No one can remember what kind of guitar I was strumming that April afternoon at the 35th (auditioning for Cap), but it's etched in my memory forever. I was new in-country, and yet I was getting a chance at the "gig of a lifetime." All I had to do now was execute.

After getting the thumbs up from Cap, the band and I were to be ready to go out to our first gig … the Cambodian border. We were going out to entertain an Infantry unit, (the 23rd, I think) on the edge of *hell*. We were gonna' jam for some GIs who were nervous and on their way out to look for "Charlie," and you could cut the tension with a butter knife.

As we loaded up and got ready to chopper out, you could hear the swoosh of Huey chopper blades going round and round and the sound of frags, grenades, and M-16 ammunition in the background. We were heading out to a border town near Loc Ninh.

The heat was blanketing, and the humidity was smothering. I didn't know what to think, but I knew one thing: the conditions might have been funky, but I HAD A GIG! There was uneasiness as we were about to embark on Fire Base Mary Ann, for a noon show, in the heat, with no over-hang. I kept looking over at my guitar. It made me feel better. And just to think, a year ago, I was doused in English Leather with a prom tux on, getting ready for "Grad Night." As we neared the spot and got closer to the strip, I started to sweat. It was scary.

"This is nerve-racking," the drummer murmured.
"Who lives like this, as a teenager?" he asked.
\We got closer, and over the radio came—
"You guys here?"
"That's affirmative," said the pilot.
"OK, we'll be right out. Hold on."
The ground guy says.
"Sending a couple guys over now."

What songs would we play? Would we remember the arrangements, like in rehearsal? The band was looking cool, but we were very green, and fearful. Everyone was running on adrenaline! Hey, we were just out here to play some rock 'n' roll for a bunch of *grunts*, right? I wished that someone could have filmed this, but all we got were a few pictures … and we were lucky to get those. The air was full of testosterone and gun powder, and as I sat there, I became philosophical. I started analyzing the situation again and again.

SIDENOTE: After TET of '68, the North Vietnamese, and Viet Cong came up with a new strategy. They decided to slow the war way down and saturate the South with various drugs, alcohol, and women. Later, I found out that they shipped it back to the states hidden in pine boxes and other vehicles—often in the corpses themselves - All for profit.

The chopper approached. It scared the shit out of everyone as they tried to put her down. There was so much dust you could hardly breathe. We looked at each other and our eyes said it all.
"Where the heck are we?"

Rockin' Nam

There was a lot of commotion as the pilot tried to find a place to land. I was pretty- much deaf by now, I wondered if my music was going to be jeopardized from this little excursion. My whole chakra was pretty rocked. However, I *DID* manage to hear a soft, gentle voice in all this mayhem. It seemed there was someone right behind me. She whispered to me.

"You'll do great."

I turned slightly. Whoa, the DONUT DOLLY!

Her name was Amy, and she *was* a doll! I sure did have an instant crush on her.

I answered back…

"Yeah, ya think?"

She nodded and smiled. You could tell this girl was interesting, cute, and intelligent … which is a combination boys have always been attracted to, and I was no different. I was so taken by her, it wasn't funny. She had all the qualities I was looking for. I became coyly brash …

"Yeah, and what do I get if I DO rock it?" I answered.

"Probably another gig," she spewed back playfully.

"Good one," I mused.

"So, if I *do* kick some butt and rock the house, can I have a date with you tonight?"

"I go to bed early," she retorted.

"So do I … sometimes," I said with a smile.

She continued … "I've known you for about 30 minutes now, and I can tell that you are probably really good at what you do and that's just what you were hired for. I gotta tell you, it's just what these boys need. I'll bet you're going to make them get up and take notice!"

Oh man, I liked this girl.

"Thanks for the stimulating talk. Glad I met you."

She grinned tentatively but warmly. This is what I really dug about her. She seemed so sharp, and hip, and playful. I was walking on air...giddy as a school girl that I met this one. Can she be real? Like a ton of bricks, it dawned on me,

"I think I just met the most wonderful woman in the world ... I mean I just met somebody really fabulous ... like in the movies. Was I hallucinating or was this real? Oh well. Time will tell. There's still a whole lot of show to do, but if ALL the Donut Dollies are like *this*, there are going to be some very happy GIs over here.

SIDENOTE: It never occurred to me how valuable the Red Cross volunteers were to the GIs overseas. It didn't take long for me to see that these women were a great asset to the soldiers from Dong Ha to Can Tho. I would eventually see the entire picture during my time and travels in the coming year.

The terrain was annoying. We were sitting there sweating, coughing. As the chopper was preparing to touch down, you could hear explosions, yelling, and mayhem. As we touched down, I waved goodbye to Amy, and realized how lucky I was to meet her. I was really hoping to run into her again, somewhere down the road. She was surely a diamond in the rough.

"You guys get out here! ... Kick some ass!"

Just then, two guys rushed over and helped out. They grabbed the gear. *WOW—ROADIES!* Everyone seemed good as the band arrived to play. This was a great start. Everyone out there was very accommodating.

After all, who could forget those pessimistic "A-holes" back at the snack shop. These guys had a harsh tour of duty out here. Most of them were pretty stoic. They didn't know *WHAT* to make of us. We were wondering if our guitars were going to melt. One of the band members commented,

"Hot enough for ya?"

"Welcome to 'the Nam,'" another said.

"How long do we play?" I murmured.

"An hour, I think," Chicano says.

We knew what we had to do. I took a big deep breath and proceeded to turn it up. I felt a little weak. Luckily, I'd played enough gigs to reach for something extra when I needed to. The band was a little half hazard at first, but we pulled it together quickly.

First; a nice rendition of the Doors' "Roadhouse Blues." Next, Buddy Miles, "Them Changes," followed by Creedence, "Have you ever seen the rain," and so on. The guys were remembering their rehearsals. We did well. A few soldiers were milling around. Some had acknowledged us with a few head nods and some smiles, but that was about it. They had another agenda.

A nice moment came when I happened to glance over only to notice a few of the soldiers (who were trying to concentrate on the business at hand), moving to the music. They glanced over the band's way and started bopping their heads and digging to the music.

THAT MEANT A LOT TO ME.

These infantry guys out here were getting ready for hell. They were all psyched up in different ways, passing us with occasional thumbs up. Some of them gave a head nod. It was a pretty strange setting. A few soldiers had mud on their faces. Some were crazy looking but they were all primed and psyched to go do what they had to do. They all had an attitude and wore their OD (olive drab) green camouflage uniforms. They had those attitudes I'm guessing they *had* to have.

"What a jungle!"

I was thinking to myself.

"No FUCKIN' way I could have taken an assignment like this!"

"*This* kind of job was not for me…not in a million years. Thank the Lord for not forcing me into a situation that would have possibly been fatal."

Guys were jumping up and down, twisting, grunting, barfing. The band got some notice, but the GIs' hearts and minds, as well as their attention span, were elsewhere.

We played an hour, and it wasn't all that pretty, but we *did* finish our set. It was more like a dress rehearsal for the future than anything else. I barely made it to the end of the set, and when it was over, I felt like I was going to keel over. I was *so* sick; I believe I was flirting with a serious heat stroke. The guys in the band wandered off to the mess tent. I crawled to the shade a few feet away. No one knew it, but I was in very bad shape—NO SHIT! I was on the edge—not good. I couldn't even move to get a cup of water. If I needed to go to the latrine or walk anywhere, I would have been "SOL." I *did*, have just enough strength to crawl slowly over to the awning.

I somehow made it to the Quonset hut, to a semi-shaded spot, and sat absolutely motionless. I was going to sit there forever if that's what it took. I closed my eyes and dozed off. I'm not sure how long I was out or what I was dreaming about.

A few minutes later, I awoke and felt slightly better, *slightly*. I can't remember a time I had ever pushed the envelope this hard—physically. I was a little insecure about it, to say the least. Was I *THAT* much of a wimp? I couldn't believe how hot and sick I was. I felt helpless but tried not to make it too obvious. After a while, I started to feel a little more normal. I went into the latrine and washed my face with cold water.

I came back out and sat back down in the shade for a bit. Man oh man, I thought I was in shape and could handle shit like this, but I guess I was wrong.

Finally, a passing GI stopped to comment ...

"Hey, thanks, you brought us back for a while," he said.

"Good to hear," I said with a half a smile.

I tried to act normal, trying to mask my weakness. Others walked by and smiled with a "thumbs up." I'd smile back, as I tried to seem genuine. If this all sounds dramatic, it was. I must have come off as a complete snob at times, but it wasn't like that at all. I really *did* appreciate every compliment. But at that moment, that was the best I could do. Finally, this one dude sat down.

"Good stuff man, been playin' long?"

"Since I was eleven," I said faintly.

"Outstanding ... thanks for the tunes."

You OK?" he asked.

Yeah, I'm OK. I'll survive, just a little heat stroke," I laughed.

"Where you from?" I asked.

"Oh sorry, I'm Pat from Jersey."

"Hey, I'm Flyn ... from Thousand Oaks."

I said it pretty weakly. I was trying to be as normal as possible.

He commented back.

"You're too good, how'd you wind up here? Where'd you come from?"

"I showed them I could play," (slightly sarcastic).

"Be careful what you wish for, huh?" he said laughingly.

"Well, we're sure glad you came out. Gotta run … keep on rockin', OK?" he said.

I mustered up a—

"Thanks Pat, you too."

After he left, I finally found some strength, slowly got to my feet, and muttered under my breath.

"Boy that was a close one. Thank you, Jesus!"

This was only our first gig, and already we had experienced more in forty-eight hours than some guys go through in a year. I finally wandered over to the mess hall to find the guys. I browsed at the food. There sat some old dried-up mac' and cheese, and the cheese was stuck to the plates. (If I was hungry at all before, I lost my appetite when I saw this "ca-ca"). I decided to inquire about some soup. That was the only thing that sounded good, *and* it was a safe bet. The other guys spotted me. I was trying to be casual but I think my emotions were hanging out.

"Where you been? We ate already … you want something?" Chicano asked.

"Yeah, you hungry? … maybe a little something?" asked the drummer.

"I'm telling you the truth; you look like shit. What happened to you?" Chicano asked.

Not wanting to get busted for being a wimp, I finally answered,

"No, it's OK, I'm good. Actually, do they have any soup? I'm kind of hungry," I remarked.

"So where *were* you, really?" Chicano asks.

"Signing autographs," I joked" (Big laughs).

One of guys yelled over to the cook, and he brought over a little cup of chicken noodle soup. The cooks had gotten wind of the band and how good we were. They were happy to accommodate. It was nice to hear that. I wish I could have eaten, but at this point, I could only handle the soup. The guys were done eating and just stared at me with a big grin that reflected just what I was about to say.

"HEY, WE MADE IT THROUGH OUR FIRST GIG!' I boasted.

I was embarrassed to tell them the truth—how I was such a lightweight, sitting motionless by myself for an hour, trying to act normal.

"You good?" Chicano asked

"I'm good … spaced out, apparently," I said with a laugh.

"I heard that," said the drummer.

We had some time to kill, and I had a little more energy now. We sat around and chatted with some of the guys. Most of them were pretty burnt. They were hardcore but complimentary. Their nerves were callused and numb. They weren't the type to fawn all over us. Finally, it was time to head back to Cam Ranh.

We walked away from the firebase feeling fairly good about everything. We felt like we did the job and THEN some. Now it was time to gather our shit and get to the chopper. We loaded back into the Huey again, and headed for the 35th.

As I got on board, I noticed a new crew at the helm. I had clearly started to feel normal again. In fact, I was feeling so good; I started to get a little antagonistic. I decided to mess with them a little more, to push the envelope ... ask ballsy questions. I tried to be subtle and I leaned over and whisper but I'm sure everyone heard me.

"Soooo, where's Amy?"

One pilot stared at the other for a few seconds, and then they both looked away. It was pretty goofy. After all, I was still a cherry *AND* my rank was still that of a private...and probably most importantly...
I WASN'T SUPPOSED TO BE INTERESTED IN ANY OF THE RED CROSS WORKERS!!!

Overall I had a lot of nerve. I didn't get an answer. I pondered asking again but thought better of it. Instead, I just put my head back and closed my eyes to take a snooze. Got to rest up for the gig on Saturday night, an important night for sure.

We finally landed, and I decided to take a parting shot as I continued my quest to check up on my favorite Donut Dolly. As we got out, I started to fuck with the crew once again. I couldn't help it, but they were an easy mark.

"OK, well ... then ... say hi to Amy for me." I said, with a shit-eating grin on my face.

I thought I heard them answer, but I couldn't be sure with all that noise from the chopper.

What they probably *really* said was,

"Yeah, we'll be sure to do that for you ... or, what a smart-ass. This guy is a real character," they said.

So after almost going down the tubes, I now walked with a spring in my step. I had done a "180" and was now back to 100 percent.

Rockin' Nam

As we settled back in to the hooch, the big gig was only two days away on Saturday night. We knew what we had to do and we wanted to prove it to Cap and his friends, to show some gratitude for what he'd done for us, the gigs. So now we were gonna rock out and relax and kick back with wine, women and song...I knew what I had in mind and it's just what the doctor ordered. Ironically, after spending quite a while sinking so low, I was thinking that, unbelievably, I now found myself, sitting on top of the world!

The following week came quickly. We went over some tunes that needed tweaking, started learning a couple new ones. Kim our housekeeper (hootchkeeper) and I started getting pretty cozy. There was a convoy leaving early Wednesday morning for Phan Rang. We had a gig at 7:00 p.m. that night. The band wasn't totally comfortable getting up that early but like a bunch of celebrities, we headed out on the next leg of the tour to yet another engineer battalion a couple hours away.
There were several GIs on the convoy for myriad reasons. I don't remember many of the details, but I'm pretty sure no one knew there was a band on board.
We arrived in Phan Rang, late afternoon. It was a small village on the water southeast of Cam Ranh. I never really got into Phan Rang, but it was an important 3rd step for us. The night was fairly uneventful. The soldiers were cordial and pretended to be cool, but the energy and excitement level was pretty low, as they showed us to our quarters...More comedy from yours truly...
"Another day, another dollar," I joked.
"Don't you just love it," replied Chicano.

We got ready for the show, happy that we were able to work in a couple new tunes because *this* was the perfect place to try them out. Some of the soldiers were glad that there was going to be some entertainment, but most of the GIs seemed apathetic. It was like they were bored and burnt out and struggling with their time there. They all seemed pretty tired and ready to go home. The band kidded each other that the publicist might have dropped the ball on this one. However, I was quick to take into consideration that these guys had seen their share of clone bands and other copy cats. There were many reactions, mostly good. The band and I took it in stride, and we did our best. After the show, a couple of the guys were worn out and went to bed early.

I hung out for a while and talked to some of the guys, but it wound up getting late, so I wandered off to some hooch. I didn't get to sleep right away. This whole thing was such a whirlwind. It was hard to process how wild and crazy everything was. As I lay in bed, I stared out for a while.

The next morning, we caught another convoy. This time it was to another "sister company", the 577th Engineer Battalion in Don Duong (Pronounced Don Zoom). The area was unique because it was up in the Central Highlands. So right off the bat, it was going to be cooler. It was very rich in French influence and, as we would find out later, it wasn't far from Dalat, the infamous, gorgeous French city with cobblestone streets high atop the Langbian Plateau. Dalat was, apparently, French for ..."Dalat! It was one of the most beautiful cities in all of Vietnam. It was a resort town for the soldiers and locals alike. It was very cool most of the year, and even snowed a little in the winter.

It was French through and through. The so-called story goes that the French came to 'Nam before WWII but lost it to Ho Chi Minh. They hung around in the South after the '54 accords, but left for good after '56. When the US got the bright idea to send advisors into the country in '58, the French begged us not to go in. They told us it'd be a "dead-end street," a no-win situation, but someone in the State Department saw too many dollar signs to heed that warning, no matter how many lives it cost. This subject would become a hot item, a great bone of contention for years to come.

Dalat was about an hour farther north, up in the highlands. I would get to visit Dalat a little later when I had free time to wander. We pulled into the 577th engineer battalion and it felt good. The vibe was great. We went to set up. We all grabbed some grub and started to schmooze with the guys. You could tell this was to be a great gig by the way they all acted. I was elated to hear that, unbelievably, some of the guys had heard of us—

We got to set up in a great space, and the sound was kick-ass. Some of the soldiers brought chairs in. The place packed up. I looked at Chicano and gave him that grin that just about said,

"Man this is gonna be fun ...."

For the first time in four gigs, the GIs came in early and waited with anticipation. We had done a sound check, and the pieces were in place. The room was abuzz. What a change from the previous gig, like night and day. We were pumped! This was going be our night!

The roof was about to come off the EM club at the 577th!

We opened with a new tune, "Vehicle" (Ides of March). From there, we flew through the show like a breeze. Some guys sat there with their mouths open. Others, mesmerized, the set that night was the best we'd had done so far. They were really digging the tunes. We went to another level, the more the crowd rose with us. This was the best. The band dug the crowd that we actually kicked it into a higher gear. The more we rocked the better. We settled into a great groove. We gained a lot of confidence after the firebase show, and it showed. Nothing much else mattered at the moment. Everything clicked. Finally, it looked like our efforts, our rehearsals, maturity in-country, were paying off.

This was as some describe as a, "killer gig." We even threw in that Chuck Berry tune we used for the encore the previous weekend. Meanwhile, I discovered something new about these gigs. It would be something I'd look forward to from here on out—THE AFTER PARTY! Yes, that quality time with the guys after the gig.

After the show, we must have talked for hours. It eventually got to be 12 or 1 a.m. It seemed we could have gone all night, but the guys had been up since early morning—so off to bed. We had to travel back the next day, and the Don Duong guys had jobs in the morning. We shut it down for the night. It was a great end to a great trip.

The next morning came way too early. We packed up and started to head out. It was hard to leave such a great place. Still on cloud nine from the night before, everybody was high-fiving and smiling, and before we left, I vowed to come back soon. (Who knew I'd be so prophetic?). I'm sure to this day, we all remember that gig.

Rockin' Nam

When we returned to Cam Ranh, we felt very good. We were partying and celebrating. We were like a giddy bunch of school girls, laughing and cackling all the way back to the 35th!

Back at Cam Ranh, the "party hooch" was in full swing. Even while the band was gone, the posse still hung out at the hooch and entertained all the GIs going north and south. Now that we were back, even MORE guys came around—some of the local girls came around also. Kim, our maid, was still stopping by every morning to say "hello" and a visit for a few minutes before she had to go to work. She did everyone's laundry and was very sweet. We liked each other, but I wasn't ready for anything serious.

I liked to go into my room and relax, listen to tunes. I went in and cranked up some tunes, and just kicked back. It must have been less than five minutes, and I was conked out. I don't know how long I slept, but when I got up there was a houseful (or is that a "hoochful?"). We gabbed and partied and spent time running down some songs. A couple mornings later (little bit of a bummer), we woke up to find that someone had snuck into the pad in the middle of the night and lifted the bass guitar ... So, BING—no bass! What do we do now? The two of us went to the Cap and told him. Chicano and I had concocted this ridiculous scheme to get permission to go and buy a bass guitar and other needs. We needed to take a couple days and go to Saigon! We told Cap that he should send us down there to buy a bass and some other things we needed. We were out of music supplies. The stuff we needed wasn't close by...a bass, some picks, strings, drum sticks, basically your general laundry list for a working band.

And the SHOCKER! Without much hesitation, he said, "OK!"

"Whoa! He said YES! "

So, in the blink of an eye, the bass player, and I got our shit together and got our asses to the airport. We were off to the big city. *AND!* It was a business trip! It didn't even cost us an R & R (every GI got one R & R (a week-long vacation, anywhere, in a twelve-month cycle).

Vietnam was a different country, but IT WAS THE ARMY! We'd wear civilian clothes, NOT army junk! We'd be enjoying this new country like jet-setters. Chicano and I had gotten pretty close in a very short time. Of course, it seemed like nearly everyone got very close very quickly. It was just something that was definitely a fact.

SIDENOTE: My friend demanded to be called Chicano. I I don't think I never even knew his real name. He was very talented. I often wonder where he is today. He was from my home state—A Latino from La Puente! Which was a suburb and not too far from Los Angeles. He was confident and had a great smile. When he wasn't hangin' with us, he liked to hang with the brothers. We had a lot of fun together.

In Saigon, we were two soldiers on the prowl. Chicano was cool. He grew up in East L.A. (different than Thousand Oaks). He was a good bass player and an incredible carpenter. He single-handedly built all the rooms at the hooch and made any improvements we requested. It was like our own personal condo back home, very cool.

We bonded with the cabbie, and it didn't take long to hook us up with a couple of local girls to help show us around. We both spent time playing tourist, and going out and about with girls and were having a wild time, not thinking about much else. It turned out to be a fun weekend but it was time to get back. Oh yeah, we *DID* manage to get the supplies we needed (a bass, picks, and strings etc.).

We headed back to Cam Ranh. There we sat, with burned-out expressions on our faces. We were drained! Dead tired! A lot of crazy thoughts were dancing in our heads. We were both anxious to get back and do some jamming. We were like two crazed dogs coming back. After several nights out chasing it and getting' wild, we were ready to get back to the hooch. We were drained.

"Those guys at the 35th are not going to believe it," I told homeboy. "It seems like an eternity since we'd been home," I told him.

"It'll be good to get back … play again," he said.

When we returned, I was pretty spent. I was moving slowly and trying to make my way around. I went to the pad. There was no one there. There *was*, however, a note on the door: ***Come see Cap right away!*** ***I HAD A BAD FEELING ABOUT THIS!***

It felt strange. I was feeling kind of psychic. I knew this wasn't good at all. When I got down to the office, it was just as I suspected! BAD NEWS —VERY BAD NEWS! None of us realized it at the time, but, as we returned to the party hooch, we'd already played our LAST GIG. I got down there and two officers were sitting in the office: my Cap and some pompous-looking major.

Sadly, the captain explained to me that while we were gone, a high-ranking major had come through and immediately deemed the hooch "unacceptable" and ordered the whole thing shut down—ASAP. This guy had no idea how talented we were. He had no idea how much joy we brought to those soldiers out in the field.

Apparently, a Major Needlewick was on his way to somewhere when he discovered the party hooch. He was shocked at the goings-on…All the shenanigans "illegal" activity—the drugs, the girls, and so forth.

"I want it down! I want it down now!" he commanded. "It is to end, effective NOW!

I was livid … I couldn't believe it. I didn't know whether to be pissed or break down.

"Isn't there anything we can do, Cap?" I pleaded.

"I'm a rocker...don't know how to do anything else!"

"Sorry soldier, he has his orders," the major snorted.

I stared at the major.

"His ORDERS?" I shot back. "What about the needs of the GIs who count on the music to make their day?" I demanded. "What are you gonna do now...to entertain the troops? Just go back to cranking up some more golden oldies on those shitty speakers!"

"Careful, Private!" Cap warned.

"What? You're joking right? We kicked ass out there! And you're going to just shut it down? Like that?"

"You don't need to carry that tone with me, soldier!" Needlewick slams.

"You think you're a rocker, son?"

"No! Private, **HERE**, you're a soldier!"

"**HERE**, you have a job to do!"

"You're a million miles away from LA! You got it? Now that's an order, and that's the end of it!"

"Well, that's NOT the end of it!" I said.

"I'm sorry. Now, if there's nothing else," he said.

"Yeah, I'll bet you are," I snapped back.

"Well, I'm not staying here! I'M NOT GOING TO TYPE OR MAKE COFFEE! After the ride I've been through? How can I possibly go backwards like that? Are you insane?" I screamed.

Cap was also pissed. After all, his ass was on the line too.

"Really? What do you have in mind? To go AWOL?" he posed.

"Yeah! send me out—away from here!" I yelled. The major stepped in …"And just where would THAT be?" he shot back.

"I don't know … maybe out to the 'bush'?" Somewhere far away, that's for sure!"

"In fact, how about one of the places I just was?" I demanded.

"I'll write songs, lay in the sun … change the world from there!"

"You can't just write your own ticket," he said.

He was now getting madder.

"And you're not going to order me around." "I'M NOT YOUR TRAVEL AGENT!" he screamed.

He was getting more and more steamed by the minute. The major looked at me with scorn. He was pissed. Finally he'd had enough. He stormed out.

"Send me now, Cap! Please!"

Cap and I had always liked each other. We had an odd relationship, but a good one. However, now he was "feelin' it," mostly because of this situation.

It was uncomfortable for him and after all, he was still my commanding officer. It was ugly ... and getting uglier. (Who I really think Cap was mad at was that dickhead, Needlewick, the guy who ordered us shut down.

He never even heard the band or saw a show and he comes marching in and starts to give orders.

"Get me out of here, Cap," I said calmly.

"OK, you got it," You wouldn't be any use to me now anyway, especially after this. OK, you're gone."

Full of grief and despair, I headed back to the hooch for a last look-around. I started getting sick as a dog. I took one last look around. I was now on my way out, on my way out to the cool of the mountains.

Out to the Central Highlands where, just a couple weeks ago, I'd been a "rocker" playing one of my best gigs! Once a celebrity in Don Zume, I was now to be a mere soldier, ready show up as a lowly private, sick from depression and mad as hell. Little by little, those hanging around were just hearing about this, and they felt for me. The last thing I remember was the mood at the band hooch. Sadly, it ends. It was very, very somber...depressing. I recall, as we all cleaned up and cleared out, it was like a morgue. As fast as it started, it came to a screeching halt.

SO, *THE BAND DISSOLVES.*

No one knew where the others were going. The paradise I'd known was all gone.

There were duffle bags on the trucks with no guitars. There were no amps on their way out ... NO itineraries, and NO "music tours" going anywhere; just back to the regular Army life. Just ordinary soldiers ready to travel to parts unknown—and me, sadly, I was on my way out for re-assignment.

Rockin' Nam

So many questions went through my mind ... A lot of "What-ifs." What if the bass hadn't gotten stolen? What if the major had actually *SEEN* the band perform? I was soooo depressed; I needed help. This was huge—the band, the memories—all weighing pretty heavy on my mind. The tragedy was that it seemed like we were just getting started, just getting our rhythm.

I couldn't believe how it all went down. Just as everything was beginning to bloom, it all crashed. Was our karma catching up with us for being so out of control? What a situation! I hadn't been in country but a couple of months, and already I'm up against it. What do I do? I only had myself to blame. The next few days were critical for me. I remembered those last moments in Cam Ranh. I sat, depressed and heart- broken. I knew I'd probably get in trouble for this, but I couldn't think about that now. I was just concentrating on living one more day. If I could just survive another day, I know I'd be okay. I gazed at my bed one more time ... my hammock ... the walls where my black-light posters were ... the bed where I slept—very sad. What do I do now! Shit. Where there were once such great memories ... now, only painful ones.

I NEVER SAW ANYONE FROM CAM RANH AGAIN!

Oh well, I guess all good things must come to an end!

Rockin' Nam

BAND ON THE RUN
4.

I *arrived at my new post* (the 577th Engineer Battalion in Don Duong (pronounced Don Zoom) and it was ironically, just weeks after the band and I rocked and brought the house down. This was going to be very uncomfortable for me. One minute I'm a "rock star," the next, I'm a lowly private showing up for duty. The base was very blue collar—no room for celebrity and the guys up there were all business. What, in the world, was *I* going to do? I could hardly move from the drugs I took during my meltdown in Cam Ranh. I was like a kid. Got my gig taken away, the band, the hooch, the tour—everything was gone, so I threw a hissy fit.   I got out there, and was pretty sick. A few of the guys recognized me right away. They were quick to help me, to hide me, to get me soup and water. (Even the staff Sergeant in charge was cool). I just had to settle down and recuperate for a few days before checking in. I knew I'd hear it from Cap for being late. However, getting my health back was a priority. Everything else took a back seat. Now officially AWOL, I spent time laying on the bottom of somebody's bunk and hurting for hours at a time. By this time, the guys at the 577th had heard the story and most of them were on my side. I won't ever forget what great camaraderie I had as a member of the unit during my time there. As it turns out, these guys were the best!

When I finally *DID* check in, the CO was perplexed with my tardiness but didn't make a big deal out of it. My reputation had preceded me, and he told me I was just going to have to play "Army" for a while. (It would be the first time since I arrived in- country that I'd have to work a "straight" job). One thing I noticed, Don Duong wasn't the same place as I knew before. This time I *wasn't* the center of attention. In fact, I was actually a "nobody" and I... DIDN'T KNOW HOW TO DO ANYTHING! I was a musician!

The new Cap was going to put me to work, but doing what? ...and where? What could I do? How could *I* be any help to them? He wound up putting me in charge of the motor pool, a place where the trucks would gas up in the morning and I'd do other various vehicle-related functions.

I was a little embarrassed at first, but I fell in. It felt strange, working, rather than playing. I always had the feeling that it would be short-lived. For now, I filled trucks up with Shell diesel and guarded my post. This was all very different for me but after awhile, I was okay with this new-found leisure. It gave me time to think and relax...AND GET WELL. I got to go into the "Ville" (local village) pretty much whenever I wanted to and I went in almost at will.

I wound up spending more and more time down there with "Mama-san," along with some of my new buddies. She was very cool. She always had some pot and some girls. She'd put out fresh-cut oranges and there were always a few GIs around.

As I made my way around the "Ville", I thought to myself,

"Hard to imagine, there's a war going on."

Rockin' Nam

These days of my "Nam experience" were like no other. No tour, no deadlines, and I had nothing but time on my hands. I'd often hang and bullshit with everyone.

I'd while away the time, dream of playing music again, and continue to talk about my future plans. This would be the only stretch of my year that I'd have this kind of idle time. In fact, I was so idle, that I actually took a Vietnamese language class once a week. Did this attractive 30-something Vietnamese teacher have anything to do with it? Probably, but I DID learn how to speak a little.

As I got more comfortable at the pump, I started to get bored. I should never have time on my hands, especially with a little money in my pocket. It was a recipe for disaster and it's a miracle I never got in *real* trouble or worse, anything fatal. *That* would have been ugly ... to eat it, and get sent home in a pine box but not from anything "war related?"

Similar things did happen to certain people. There was talk about a guy getting bit by a rat one night and sent home with a medal. Another guy fell off a swift boat into the South China Sea, down in the Delta region.

He supposedly hurt himself, so they shipped him out with accommodations. However, before he left, he went back, took a camera, and filmed himself in a recreation of the incident for his own future promo. Rumors were that, years later, he ran for office.

With all the distractions that came while I was on the prowl, I should have gotten in "BUKU" trouble. I got no accommodations...no Purple Hearts nor distinguished medals, but I *DID* get lucky ... I came back with enough memories for a lifetime.

Rockin' Nam

Certain parts of the country were ideal for the partying GI ... the sun, the girls, cigarettes, powder, playing guitar, and schmoozing with the guys. Other parts were kind of "ho-hum," and ripe for mistakes.

I probably got in more trouble than the average bear, but I had fun doing it. I came close to disaster quite often, and very close to ruining my "good time," but I was lucky and fortunate, to say the least. Can you say, "Living on the edge?" Later on, I would try and act right, but I never quite came around to that concept completely. It was just so much more fun to take chances.

One day, Gibo and I decided to take a few of the kids to the beautiful French city of Dalat, a few miles away. We had wanted to see this city for a while now. It was the town with the cobblestone streets and the beautiful French architecture. It had a great reputation throughout with soldiers and townspeople alike.

We were going to have a beer and get the kids some ice cream. It was just as advertised...gorgeous. I was thinking,

"This must have been the pride of the French ... when they were here, in Nam."

It was such a beautiful town, loads of culture. We headed out on a sunny afternoon and bummed a ride on a couple rickety vehicles that were clinking and clanking as they went down a gravely, stony, dirt road. We pulled into a place that had a little of everything—ice cream, beer, cigs, et cetera. The kids got their cones, and Gibo and I decided to chill out with a couple of beers. After all, it seemed like a fairly innocent thing to do on a nice, warm, sunny day, as we were looking forward to this.

As we sat chatting and joking, I looked around, and I was taken aback. I had noticed that some of the soldiers in the place weren't ARVNS (South Vietnamese soldiers). They were more like NVA or VC (Viet Cong). I didn't freak. After all, we were all just having a friendly beer. I caught the eye of one of the military-clad soldiers. We stared at each other and then, in a shocker, the guy raised his beer can. I slowly raised mine. Was that a Kodak? Toasting with the enemy! This would have been quite a story in the "Stars and Stripes," not to mention the shit-storm it would have caused around the compound. I don't even want to think about it. Just then, a couple MPs (military police) came in and ambled over to us. I leaned over and told Gibo, "Uh oh, look out now."

We both laughed as they walked over and approached us.

"What are you guys up to?" they asked.

"Nothing," said Gibo ... "just taking kids for ice cream."

"Got any papers?" one of them asked.

"Man, we're just doing a solid for the kids," I explained.

"So ... no papers?" they demanded.

"C'mon, bro ...," I argued.

"I'm not your bro, bro. Step outside, by the jeep."

"SHIT, I muttered. Can we finish our beers?"

"No, you may not," said the other one, emphatically.

"Well ... then can we buy you guys a couple ice-water enemas?" I asked.

Gibo started cracking up. Now they were pissed! They proceeded to handcuff us and lock us up. No, not in a jail or anything ... no, they locked us up in a steel box! They took us to a cargo box called a "Conex."

A Conex is a huge, steel storage crate that once housed weapons, ammo, or other supplies. They put the two of us in and LOCKED THE DOOR! Can you imagine that? If they would have done that today, what kind of hell would it raise? We didn't freak out. In fact, we just took it in stride. We settled in and sat in the dark steel box and chatted 'till we got tired. I was thinking ...

"Is this what you get for doing a favor for the kids?"

Gibo and I survived the night in the "box" but we were pretty spaced out on the way back. He and I didn't say much, but I know he was thinking pretty much the same thing I was—FTA ("F" the army). It was a familiar mantra around the Nam.

Back at the compound, there was rarely a dull moment. I didn't spend a whole lot of time in the Central Highlands, but what time I DID spend, I made every moment count. It was amazing. It seemed that, as the war sorry, *conflict*, wore on. Washington would start spending more time analyzing situations and nitpicking. They would try to make our lives more and more difficult with their petty rules. (sound familiar?)

It all came down in the spring of '71. The State Department FINALLY caught on to the "drug" problem that was spreading all over South Vietnam. They sent a Senator Fulbright over to investigate the "problem" in country.

After only two days in Saigon, as he's walking down the main drag in Saigon, some boy-san approaches and asks him if he wants to buy some "stuff." That was it!

And thus starts the military's way of dealing with the problem … by closing all access to the "Villes." Ah, the Army way … SHUT IT ALL DOWN! …Shut it down? Typical Army, don't address it, just kill it.

It started out as an ordinary weekday morning. I finished my chores and decided to take a trip out to the bush with the guys. I had a beat-up guitar, and they were on their way out to lay down some tar.

Of all my days in "The Nam," this day, in particular, stood out as one of the "classics." It was an afternoon for the ages on a cloudy day in the spring. It was something none of us will ever forget.

I finished gassing up the last vehicle, grabbed the guitar, and jumped on board. I didn't know it but I was going to be in for the ride of my life! Earl was the driver. He had very long hair and was from Michigan— Dearborn, I think. He was a quiet leader. Everyone had a lot of respect for him. When Earl smiled, he lit up the world. I jumped in his truck; my guitar strapped across my back and I said,

"Let's go jam."

He gave a big smile and drove on.

On this particular morning, the crew was on their way out to a quiet, desolate mountain spot known as the Montagnard area.

The Montagnard people were like the American Indian … from the same area but living in their own protected space. They were able to take care of their own and guard their own territory. They were also very creative, self-sufficient, artsy. The kids were great. They made gold bracelets and beaded necklaces.

They handed them out to the guys…lots of wrist bands too. The Montagnard kids were so artistic.

Rockin' Nam

FEBRUARY, 1971

They were fun and creative. It wasn't that the "city" kids *weren't* fun; they just weren't quite as artistic as the mountain kids. We loved the artsy stuff they made.

We wore it with pride. The kids, mostly eight through thirteen, and were jazzed that we were there. All the guys were equally excited about the "bling" that the kids offered up. Of course, we bought lots of stuff, and gave the kids good money. We gave the families cash, and we ponied up greenbacks (worth more).

We did our best to try and make their lives better. After all, I think they all needed a break at this juncture. What happened next had to be one of the greatest highlights ever experienced in 'Nam, or anywhere else.

As noon approached, the Kids were starting to gather with their gifts. I was still jamming. In less than a minute, they had gathered 'round. For some reason, I got the crazy idea to break into a song. I don't know how it happened, but it just came to me, and seemed like a good idea. Everybody sat up as I suddenly broke into the old "60s" tune…

"I TOOK MY TROUBLES DOWN TO MADAM RUE…" and just like that, incredibly, one of the kids chimed in!

"YOU KNOW DAT GYPSY WIT' D GOLD CAP TOOTH,"
I replied,

"SHE GOTTA PAD DOWN ON 34TH AND VINE … SELLIN' LITTLE BOTTLES OF" …

All of a sudden, all the kids were in (together): *"LOVE POTION NO. 9!"*

Rockin' Nam

What an incredible experience! The guys couldn't believe it. It was almost like a dream. It was, for sure, one of the greatest moments ever!

We all spent about an hour or so with the kids. We could have stayed all day.

"One of the best times ever in 'Nam," a soldier said. Woody and Stash said it would stay with them forever. For me, it's as vivid *now* as the day it happened.

SIDENOTE: Today, GIs still have some of those beads and bracelets packed away. For me, I put them in a safe place and locked them away. Every once in a while, I'll pull them out and look at them, even put them on.

All the way back, the guys could not stop smiling about the day and as we arrived back in Don Zoom, the guys went right to their ritual (down to the water to wash their trucks to prep for the next day).

I wandered around for a while but soon found out that the captain was looking for me.

"Cap looking for you."

"Why?" I gulped.

"You'll find out."

Before I could even head over to the office, I ran into some buddies and got the word. Apparently, Cap was pissed that his "gas-pumper" was gone all day. I went over to the office.

I was feeling uneasy about this whole thing. I had a feeling I was about to be in trouble.

"Well, soldier, how was your day?" Cap sarcastically asked.

"… Out with the guys, Sir."

"To do what?" he asked rhetorically.

"… hang out … play some music."

"Well, this ain't no Carnegie Hall, son.

It's not a hootenanny or a love-in either."

He then said,

"Sorry, but I'll have to take that guitar," raising his voice.

"WHAT? NO!" I cried.

"There just ain't gonna be a 'whole lotta shakin' goin' on' out here," he demanded.

"No way, Cap … it's all I got! Even Lancaster got to have his bird at Alcatraz."

"You comparing my camp with a prison, son?" he asked. "I keep a tight ship here," he explained.

"No," I assured him … I mumbled, "Tight ship? I didn't know we were in the navy,"

"WHAT WAS THAT?" he asked.

"Oh, nothing" I said.

"Good," said Cap…"Smart ass … Have that guitar in my office in an hour, I'm not kidding." Reluctantly, I showed up and brought him the beat-up guitar. It was like prying something near and dear from my hands…bummer! What was I going to do now: play more army?

This was going to be difficult because I was only good at one thing, and it had nothing to do with the motor pool. Playing music and touring around just felt right. It was a thrill giving my fellow soldiers a reason to smile, to give them some hope for an hour or more a day with music. (I could never understand, with so few musicians around, why they were always trying to take away my guitar.)

It told me something else too. It told me that things were changing in 'Nam — again.

It went much more by the book—stricter, more "army-ish" … not a good sign. I tried to adjust, to fall in line, but I wasn't having much luck.

While I DID have a smidgen of patience left, I really had no idea JUST HOW LONG I'd have to hang out in Don Zume. Would it be forever? Some of the guys heard about the guitar incident. They were really cool. They sympathized as the rumor made its way around camp that night. One of the guys stepped up and gave me the "Info of a lifetime." It seems that an organization called SSVN (Special Services Vietnam) in downtown Saigon was holding ongoing auditions. They were booking national tours. This place was a major hub for sending out bands to tour the entire country.

This was a huge opportunity for me to go and "get back in it" … for an epic tour! To go out and tour every base in country and entertain so many soldiers would be huge.

"HOW GREAT IS THIS! … A second chance!"

The deal was that inside SSVN (Vietnam special services program), was a division called CMTS (Command Military Touring Shows), and they put bands together. My guys even had a phone number for me. They heard that there were auditions on a regular basis. I was ecstatic but leery about my situation. After all, I was stuck all the way up in the Central Highlands, fading into obscurity. I had to get out of there! I had to try and get into position, to get my chance.

I needed to get down there in person, a chance to prove myself. I knew I could seal the deal if I get down there in person. Man! Those guys at the 577th—they were the best! I remember thinking,

"Seems like wherever I went the guys were always looking out for me."

I always felt that I was so lucky to be connecting with people like these. I was lucky to have the kind of rapport I had with the guys. In Don Zume, these guys would turn out to be some of the nicest guys I'd ever meet. I built some lasting relationships and we had *SO* much fun together. Most of the people I know today could never grasp this. It's just not the same now.

Later in the day, I snuck into Cap's office and called the "Special Services" building in Saigon. I scheduled an appointment for an audition. I was a little worried about Cap finding out since things between us were already touchy and I was walking on egg shells.

If this went south, it would be another black mark and I couldn't afford to get in trouble again. I told Saigon where I was, and they said they'd send orders up ... to bring me in for an audition. I was excited — but nervous. I didn't want to get my hopes up but I couldn't help feeling like it was another great opportunity on the horizon (and to think that it was not long after the last one ended). Besides, this one was a major one!

This was going to be huge! "BIGTIME!" I was pretty desperate and ready to do anything to get out and go play some more music. Of course, Cap was going to give me a ration of shit for this. Still, I could hardly contain myself. This was important. I knew if I could get down there, I could get the gig and get back to rockin' again.

One this was certain. I was always up against it. Certain people were always trying to stop me along the way. From my parents taking the guitar away (for bad report cards), to me getting fired from the band in New

Orleans, to having to inch my way into the soldier show in Atlanta; and then there were those "jag-offs" at the snack shop; and who could forget Major Needlewick putting the kibosh on our band out of Cam Ranh. It seemed like everywhere I'd go it was the same. I guess I was never going to understand this. I was always confused at what good it did taking someone's passion away. I guess I was just going to have to fight my way through it beside, this was worth it. It was a dream I'd thought about on the way over to Nam, but doubted it would never happen. In reality, I was a gas station attendant way out in the bush with boredom at my window and apathy at my door.

All of that was about to change!

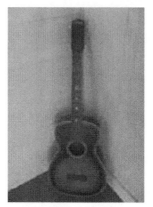

'62 Silvertone

Rockin' Nam

Fred and Alice owned Catalina Books and Records in Redondo Beach, California. Most afternoons, my brother and I would run down to the store, stand in the corner, and play and sing our hearts out.

 Uncle Bob, took me in, gave me a car and a place to stay. It was so great that he got me "in" at...Laine Enterprises. As it turns out, it was a game-changer.

My boss, Marshall Leib (Left), with his old pal, Phil.

Freeman King was a favorite around town. It was a special day when he walked into Laine Enterprises. We bonded quickly and pounded out a song in four hours. It was later published by Beachwood Music, and even later through EMI.

In 1969, after a long night in the French Quarter, I'd go to this great place and get a cup of chicory coffee and two powdered donuts for 34¢.

Basic training, Fort Polk, Louisiana in 1969… Notice the cool magazine cover in the background.

Rockin' Nam

Me and my Native buddy in "basic
training" – we played every weekend!
Fort Polk, Louisiana, '69

Rockin' Nam

Chicano
and me–
December,
1970

The girls who showed us around Saigon—Funny,
they never showed their faces in any of the
pictures we took. It got us thinking…hmm …."

Rockin' Nam

Smokin' in
the boys
'room ...

Me and the "Wood-man" (from San Diego). We
hung out at the 577th together ... hard to believe, but
the very night I got home, I went a local party in
Thousand Oaks, and guess who shows up!

Sometimes guys had too much time off and
were hilarious pretending their girlfriends
were watching them!

Rockin' Nam

There *were* places we were unable to visit…for obvious reasons.

Our housekeeper, Kim…She was a warm, loving friend … such a fun companion during my first couple months in Cam Ranh.

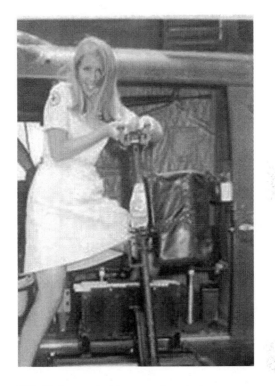

Of all the volunteers, she was my very favorite. She gave me a lot of support throughout the year … Thanks Amy!

Montagnard bling! I still have a lot of this in a box at home!

The Montagnard kids … wonderful!

One of my letters of recommendation from Laine Enterprises ... typed up and signed by Muriel, herself.

My certificate from the "soldier show in Atlanta. It was a lot of fun!

Woody —just chillin' …

With the posse, outside our party hooch.

Donut Dollies!

They were everywhere...I wasn't aware
of how much of a help they were to the
GIs until later...after I got back.
Thank you!

The Montegnard kids! The beads and
bracelets they made were beautiful!

One of the first gigs in Cam Ranh ...

Pat "from Jersey"… met him early and hung out with him a lot—good times!

…And always… the guys!!

Lotta soldiers jammin'

Ready for the road!

Viet "Bling"

Sign of the times …

New Orleans, 1969

Rockin' Nam

BACK TO THE FUTURE
5.

When I was young, I noticed the newspaper … I didn't read it … I knew about events on TV … I didn't watch it … I'd heard about Vietnam … I didn't sweat it. I guess I didn't really key in on the reality of all these things. I was in my own little world and I caught the usual shows on TV.

While I hung out with my friends, I was consumed with my band, girls, smoking, partying, and carrying on. We were digging shows like: *I Dream of Jeanne, Gilligan's Island, Bewitched,* and more … *Mr. Ed, My Favorite Martian, The Jetsons,* and so forth. I was either veggin' out or playing my guitar. However, at the same time, I **did** have angst. I wanted out! I was ready to get up and go see the world. At 18, my home town had nothing more to offer me.

After graduating, I was free to go. I was free to travel, to smoke, to have sex, to get crazy, throw caution to the wind, and get down to finding out exactly who I was. In town, I had a decent band.

We got hired to play some gigs (school dances, rotary clubs, and so forth), but it was fairly uneventful. We just didn't make **that** big of a splash. I had a couple girlfriends but they eventually dumped me. So, to sum things up, I was a bust with women, I had a mediocre band, and I wasn't very popular in school circles. I needed to make some changes.

Rockin' Nam

Southern California was a great place grow up. It was the "New frontier," (as Fagen so elegantly put it). In the beginning, we were close to the beach. The atmosphere was electric with rock 'n' roll, girls, clean, crystal-clear water, beautiful nights, and all under that warm California sun … Redondo Beach, Ca. The unpolluted life style, the spectacular aura that surrounded me (and those like me) seemed unreal. I was really affected by everything around me — including great tunes and great artists. People like Sam Cooke, Dusty Springfield, the Shangri-Las, Bobby Vee — so many and so good!

I think it's safe to say that this was a "coming of age" period for most of us — all this incredibleness. I didn't realize it at the time, but we were about to be a part of one of the most incredible metamorphoses in modern music. Let's just say that we were in a perfect position to take full advantage of a time that was just emerging as one of the greatest eras in popular American music history. Let me say that again:

WE WERE IN THE PERFECT POSITION TO TAKE FULL ADVANTAGE OF A TIME THAT WAS JUST EMERGING AS ONE OF THE GREATEST ERAS IN MODERN AMERICAN POPULAR MUSIC HISTORY!

In 4th grade, a neighbor and school chum down the block, received a gift from his father. It turned out to be a gut-stringed acoustic guitar that his dad had brought him as a present. He was kind enough to show me some chords and I caught on quickly. I fell hard. I was hooked immediately.

I really dug the guitar, the music, the songs, as well as singing. I thanked him and ran home to tell everyone the news

"I know what I want for Christmas already—a GUITAR!"

The reaction was less than enthusiastic. In fact, it was downright chilly. The answer was an emphatic NO!

"Absolutely not!" They chanted in unison—both parents.

"Who are you trying to kid?" my mother chided, "You don't even know how to play."

"I know a few chords and can learn more," I argued.

They continued...

"There's no room for loud, twangy guitars around this house; besides, your grades are bad enough," they argued.

"But I want to be just like those musicians and those bands, rockin' out! And playing those gigs! And getting popular!"

I pleaded with them ..."PLEEEESE!"

I even started singing to them (desperate as I was) ...

"Oh they're out there having fun ... in the warm California sun .... C'mon!"

It was true, I **did** just start learning how to play, but I had a good start. A few days later, I got a hold of an old cigar box (Dutch Masters, I think). I carved several grooves into it for frets and then cleverly strung six rubber bands around it. I strutted around the house all the day long, forming chords and, believe it or not, freakishly singing songs.

Rockin' Nam

I was walking around the house, singing up a storm and strumming on this … "thing."Looking back, it's funny to think of those who witnessed this particular freak show. They probably thought I was a nut case. No big deal. That sentiment would follow me around long after the "cigar box" incident! So what, if anyone thought I was weird; I was GOING to learn those chords, and I was GOING to be a rocker.

As the California leaves turned from dingy green to dingier green, we got into Halloween, then Thanksgiving, and finally Christmas (my favorite time of year). So here we go: Christmas morning 1962—my best day. My pleading and begging finally paid off. The dream came true at 6 a.m. on December 25th. The living room was packed with presents and … whoa, hiding over in the corner—my first guitar! It was a Sears Silvertone, the little sunburst one (the one with the hole in the middle). Now, I could sing and play all day. The only serious condition the folks put on me was that the school grades had to be kept up. Of course, that would eventually go south in due time. I got punished more than your average bear. Every time I looked around, I was in the doghouse.

SIDENOTE: In the future, my guitar would be taken away on more than one occasion. I didn't care. I just found a way to keep it going, like sneaking out bedroom windows and such to sneak off and play gigs. Eventually, we got a gig at the Rotary club but I was grounded for a bad report card. No problem, I just snuck out the window, did the gig, came home, and snuck back in.

The only problem was, the next day, a picture and an article appeared in the local paper! BUSTED! I didn't even have a band yet, but I was learning song after song as fast as I possibly could. I had a one-track mind…music! I hadn't had any romance to speak of, but I was sure if I kept strumming, that would come around.

Thanks to Mom, I *did* manage to finish high school, although I didn't deserve it. After all, I was just another kid in the '60s, experimenting with girls, pot, rock 'n' roll, and the rest of it. But after graduating, I decided to "get out of dodge." I split…ran away from home. It was a bit cruel, rebelling like that, but it was the only way I could escape and make it to the next level.

Growing up in Southern California and I remember getting excited about music around the age of ten. I heard my first songs playing on AM radio. I think it was, "Johnny Angel" by Shelly Fabres" and "He's a Rebel" by the Crystals. The station was KRLA (11:10 out of Pasadena). I knew right then, I was hooked.

That year, after getting guitars for Christmas, my brother and I would play every day. We couldn't put them down. Every afternoon after school, we'd grab our guitars and most days we'd race down to Catalina Music (a music and book store in Redondo Beach). We'd stand in the back of the store, singing and strumming our little hearts out. Most people thought we were a little odd, but we didn't care. The owners dug it. They store were two early hipsters, Fred and Alice. They were right out of the "Beat" generation. They were very so supportive of us and we loved hanging with them. It was a great vote of confidence early on.

We also dug guitarist, Glenn Grey, who worked there & was a member of the surf group, "The Challengers." We didn't know what we were doing, but we were figuring it out as we went along. Much to my chagrin, my parents didn't think I was ready for prime time but the very first gig we got was a graduation dance with our band, "The Silvertones," (a trio, with my brother Pat and our neighbor pal, Ken Rumrill). We did mostly Elvis and Rick Nelson stuff. The three of us played our guitars and sang up a storm. I guess you could say we were the "Dino, Desi & Billy" of our neighborhood.

The *South Bay Daily Breeze* ran a picture and a feature on us. Family and friends were thrilled. Under the band's picture it read, "Move over Beetles!" (Notice the way they spelled "Beetles?" ...too funny.) Along with Elvis and Ricky Nelson tunes, we did some surf songs and some Chuck Berry. We rocked that graduation dance!

Soon after, the folks moved us to Thousand Oaks, Ca. and my future was gonna change. Those years were also full of music as I wound up playing in a few garage bands, doing local dances, rotary clubs, private parties, and of course, the obligatory, "Battle of the Bands."

My brother and I had already played a few gigs, seen the Beatles, and recorded a demo (at H.R. studios (off Melrose) in Hollywood as we recorded our version of the Bobby Freeman hit, "Do you wanna dance" along with "Foot tapper," an instrumental we heard by the Challengers).

A little while later, we visited a taping of the TV show, *Shindig!* (A half-hour rock show featuring a host, a house band, go-go dancers, and several artists of the day).

We got to see some of our favorites, singing their hits, even though lip-synched. Later in the year, it got even better. We got to visit the set of another pop show called *"Where the Action is"*. It was a Dick Clark production, filmed on location in and around southern California. Classic! I recall going to Cornell (now named, Agoura) to see and be part of a taping in 1965.

I wound up hanging out with Barry McGuire on this day. After sitting with him and bull-shitting for a while, I asked if I could play his acoustic guitar, and he agreed. I started strumming away (I'd been playing for a couple years now). In minutes, the lead singer of Paul Revere and the Raiders, Keith Allison, came by and snatched it out of my hands.

He mumbled,

"No one said you could play MY guitar!"

Barry couldn't stop laughing ... he thought it was the hilarious.

SIDENOTE: Thirty years later, at a Christy Minstrels reunion at the Ice House in Pasadena, and I ran into Barry! I made him sit down with me. I reminded him of that summer afternoon in the mid- 60's. He died laughing ... He was so tickled that I remembered and loved that I recreated the story! He told me that was still touring and doing shows. He handed me his card and told me to stay in touch. I think I stayed in touch on social media.

After we moved Thousand Oaks, were lucky enough to be situated right down the street from a local rec center an on Saturday nights, Casey Kasem would bring out headliners. We saw the Grass Roots, the Seeds, the 5th Dimension, Sonny & Cher (when they were "Caesar & Cleo) and many more. It was like fifty cents to get in and later a dollar!

In 1966, the ULTIMATE—we got to see the Beatles at Dodger Stadium in August of '66. In the middle of the concert, George broke a string, and Paul did a soft-shoe while George changed his own string. Remember, back in the day there were no roadies.

Two years prior, as we first watched the Beatles on the Ed Sullivan show, (complete with the growling of our parents in the back ground), the very next day, at the music store, Glenn Grey, the great surf guitarist for the Challengers, (who happened to be at the store the following day) told us that there would be NO more haircuts—for anyone! —ever!—Done! Over! We were stunned and in disbelief. We immediately ran three doors down to the barber shop, and guess what? They were closed! Wow, he was right! (Of course, only later would we discover that the barber shop was closed every Monday! What a crack up).

In June of '69, I saw Janis at the Bowl, Jimi at Newport Pop (Devonshire Downs, Northridge) along with CCR, Three Dog Night, Eric Burdon, Booker T, and many more. In July, we saw Crosby, Stills, & Nash at the Greek (with Joni Mitchell as the opening act). It was CSN's first gig. They later stated at Woodstock that it was their 2nd gig and they were "scared shitless

Rockin' Nam

JULY – 1969

A couple weeks after graduation, my friend, Ott, and some guys were driving to Lake Tahoe for a summer "vacay." In the middle of the night, I packed a pillowcase full of things. When they came, I climbed out my bedroom window, and we headed for Tahoe.

The Sierra Nevada's were one of the most gorgeous spots on the planet, and I would come to embrace this more and more through the years. Today, when I smell that aroma, it takes me back…every time. However, after only a few days, the guys I went up with wanted to head back home.

"Are you shittin' me? I just left there! That's the last place I wanted to go back to."

Ott gave me the bad news. I couldn't believe what I was hearing. He says …

"Sorry, Flea."(his nickname for me).
"We've decided to head on back. I ain't gettin' in no trouble this summer."

Why were these guys in *that* big a hurry to leave, after only a few days upon our arrival? No way was I going back. I waited 18 years to get here, to gain my freedom, and I had NO intention of turning around and going back! "Jeeez, going back? Going back to WHAT?" Shaking my head as they actually left, I have to admit I was a little lonely at first but I adapted quickly. I'm guessing this was the point when it would be a "make it or break it" for me. I was about to come into my own and discover that I was a strong and free-spirited survivor.

Rockin' Nam

The beaches in Tahoe were packed with vacationers. I eventually hooked up with some hippies. A whole bunch of them were sharing a cabin for the summer (off Highway 50, across the street from KFC). I wound up sleeping on the floor. They thought I was a bit strange but they liked the way I sang and played, so, I stayed...and grew.

I was experiencing my first taste of the "summer of love."...mescaline, psilocybin ... I fell right in. But, I was naive. I was, as they say, a babe in the woods. After all, I was from the suburbs, not the city. A nice girl at the house befriended me. We got high together and cruised around town. We didn't have sex, but we did lots of things together and got close. She was patient and kind.

As summer started heading for the home stretch, there were rumors swirling around Thousand Oaks that I was lost and that I had become a freak, a drug addict, a "wretched hippie."

Also, right around this time, my image took quite a hit. Some "so-called" friends had reported to my parents that I was living with some crazies and thought I was in trouble and headed for darkness. So this was the reputation I'd acquired after being away from home for less than TWO WEEKS?! When the folks caught wind of this, they freaked. They panicked. They called on family to help. They sent a contingency out to make a trip to northern California.

They were going to try and "rescue me." After much consultation, my uncles, (along with my brother) were on their way up to the Sierra Nevada's on a morning in the grand paradise of South Lake Tahoe.

Rockin' Nam

After a night of some pot smoking and Red Mountain wine, (or was it Boone's Farm's?), I lay sleeping on the couch. Around 9 a.m., I heard a knock at the door.

"Hi, I'm … I'm looking for my brother."

I jumped up … shocked.

"ARE YOU F'N' KIDDING ME?" I thought.

I was all spread out on the couch, all blurry-eyed. The dude who answered the door, told them,

"Um … he's not here."

I was flabbergasted!

"What!? How, the *FUCK* did they find me?"

I threw my jeans on and went towards the entry way. There they were—the three of them—on the porch. I think they were expecting to see some freak crawling along the hardwood floor. (How they found the cabin is shocking in itself.)

"Hey guys" I said.

They were taken aback.

"You're alright?" one of the uncles asks rhetorically.

"Of course, I'm OK," I assured them.

"Who were you expecting, Timothy Leary?"

"Well the word on the street is that you're pretty messed up," my brother said.

In a comedic moment, I whispered,

"Did you bring any pot with you?"

Laughing out loud, I told him,

"I'm just fucking with you, man."

"OF COURSE, I'M GOOD! What do you think?" I said with a Cheshire grin.

"I've been having a nice summer."

"Everyone up here has been very cool, that is, until you show up." (Both the uncles were standing quietly in dark suits, as the roommates were freaking out) Everyone here thought you guys were NARCS!" I told them. I mean, you're in Lake F'n' Tahoe in the middle of summer and you're wearing dark tweed suits!" Besides, you've managed to freak everyone out here. This is a little cabin in the summer and everyone here is mellow just doing their own thing." I chided.

My brother was in shades and acting as hip as ever and he tells me,

"Well, we were just sent up here by some pretty concerned family members, and I'm just doing what I was asked to do, geek-face."

I smiled at him. He smiled back. We all calmed down, and they seemed to mellow out. Uncle Dick was compassionate. He told me to give him a call anytime, and that he'd be there anytime I needed him. Bob was a little harder edged but extended an offer to come live with him for a while in Brentwood (near Hollywood). I told them that I'd think about it. We exchanged pleasantries and they left. I was good to see them but an odd situation, for sure. I went back to sleep. I woke up to find that there were big "doings" down at El Dorado beach! It was a gorgeous day, the beach was packed. I brought the guitar out and serenaded until afternoon. There was a popular band around town was holding auditions for a lead singer. It was to take place at a local night club called, "Jim Burgett's Fun House." I'd been there before. One night I saw a band there called Sanpaku (they were great). A few nights later, I saw a new group from San

Francisco, a little band called "Santana." (Talk about kick-ass). That night, I thought about going for a look-see. When I got there, there were a few twenty-something's with long hair, singing their asses off. The talent was good, and I was definitely NOT in their league. I kept thinking of the visit I got from my family earlier that day. I had ideas in my head:

"Was this a good time for me to move?"

"Or would I have to go back home and make nice?"

I said farewell to Tahoe and headed out to hitchhike. It got late, and I had trouble getting a ride past Lodi, so I actually went to sleep right there on the highway…highway 99. It was the on-ramp. Young dumb and riding my thumb, that was me. But I always felt like I had an angel on my shoulder. Somebody was definitely looking out for me along the way. I was awakened at 7 a.m. by the roar of the morning traffic. I stood there for a while and finally got a ride. The lift would take me as far as Fresno.

I got dumped onto some off-ramp in 108-degree weather. I walked across the overpass and bought a very cold drink. When I returned to my spot, something very strange happened to me. It was around noon, and it was getting hotter and even harder getting a ride.

All of a sudden out of nowhere, I hear the sound of a car wildly honking from the highway below. I saw a guy waving his arms wildly from the shoulder below. In retrospect, it was a "red flag" but, of course, I was way too naïve to recognize. This dude was dressed in an un-ironed, stained, baggy old white t-shirt, and he'd seen me from below. He was yelling beckoning me to hop down. I jumped though the ice plant and trekked down the slope to his car that was pulled off on the shoulder.

"Get in! I'm headed south."

"OK," I shouted, happy to finally get a lift.

"How'd you see me?" I inquired.

"Oh, I saw you up there," he said gruffly.

I wasn't in his car two minutes when he started talking about how hot it was and touching the leg of my jeans, asking if I wasn't too hot. I started to freak; I froze up big time. I was F'n petrified.

He kept on me with the advances. He then he proposed that we go somewhere.

"Maybe we could stop for a nap."

By this time I was shakin' like a leaf.

This guy noticed that I was completely freaked out. By the grace of God, he decided to pull over and mercifully let me out—right there on Highway 99.

This could have been fatal. I truly believe the guy wanted to kidnap me and do something bad; I was sure of it. He was going to take me to a private place and do very bad things. Years later, I tried to figure out which serial killer he was.

Thankfully, not long after, another guy stopped and offered a ride. He seemed cool. He was in a beat-up "caddie" and looked like an old hippie in his forties. I was so relieved. He gave me a "white cross" (speed), and we gabbed all the way to Bakersfield. He even bought me lunch. I was speeding (white cross), so I wasn't too hungry. I just had fruit. He wound up dropping me off in Burbank. I thanked him.

Rockin' Nam

I took a cab over to Uncle Bob's (Barrington Avenue in Brentwood). I was a little stupid. I had his address and took a cab from Burbank. I think the bill was pretty steep. But Bob paid it and I settled in.

When I got to West L. A. Bob welcomed me in. He was truly "living the dream." He made me read the newspaper every day and even *TESTED* me at the end of the week! I'm not sure how much that helped, but it must have done something because Today, I claim to be a "know-it-all." Bob turned out to be a game-changer for me. I don't know how to express my appreciation for what he did to help me. If not for Bob, this story probably doesn't happen. He provided me with a maroon '65 Ford Mustang to drive, put me up in his Brentwood apartment. He then changed my life. He set me up as an intern and part-time songwriter at a music office.

The office belonged to the famous singer, Frankie Laine. It was "Laine Enterprises," a hip publishing company just across the street from the "9000 building" on Sunset Blvd. It was very close to the Rainbow bar and grill where the Roxy is today.

I was always pretty close to Bob's side of the family—the grandparents, Uncle Dick, Aunt Betty. We had lots of get-togethers. We had family reunions, birthdays, et cetera. We had wonderful Easters and great Christmas gatherings. They pretty-much all took place at the cousin's house in Malibu Lake. Everyone came … all relatives for miles.

Bob had the distinction of being the first to take me shopping at the hip, upscale clothing stores. Fred Segal (on Melrose) comes to mind … Very cool.

I was so excited to be there. I saw Goldie Hawn buying jeans! He also took me to my first movie (in Westwood). It was *Midnight Cowboy*...Great flick! Westwood was unique because films would play there, first. They showed for weeks before being released to the rest of the country. Bob also took us to the Greek Theatre for CSN's *first* gig! (Joni Mitchell was the opening act.). He had season seats, and we sat 11th row center. A few weeks later (a concert he couldn't make), he gave me two tickets to see Jose Feliciano. His friend, Iris, even let me take her brand new Corvette-Stingray to the concert! I couldn't find a date, so I went by myself. I enjoyed the concert nonetheless.

SIDE*NOTE*: Years later, Uncle Bob would eventually wind up representing the Goldman family in the O.J. Simpson trial. He appeared on CNN and other stations many times. Every time I'd turn on the tube, there was my uncle Bob. He was sitting in the courtroom agonizing through the long sessions. It was interesting but it also dragged on and on. He also did radio and things that had to do with "the trial of the century."

Frankie Laine's office was located in a little duplex house on Sunset. The office was run by Frankie's son-in-law, Marshall Leib. Yes, **that** Marshall Leib. Marshall and fellow schoolmate, Phil Spector, graduated from Fairfax High ten years earlier. Back then, they started a band called the Teddy Bears (named after the Elvis song).

Their first song, "To know him is to love him," went straight to number ONE! Thanks mostly to Dick Clark. Marshall ran the office. His friend, Dallas Smith also ran certain things. A couple years later, Dallas would go on to produce a band called "The Five-man Electrical Band" who had a hit with a song called, "Signs."

In '69, I had heard the name, Spector ("the boy genius"), those girl-group hits, but that was about it. I didn't really know what it meant. We all heard he was the 19-year-old genius.

Marshall was such a great guy ... always so kind and fair to us. I remember him pulling up every morning in one of his Ferraris. He was a big fan of the sports cars, and since his father owned a local dealership, he had quite a collection. Marshall would gather up our songs that we had recorded at the end of the day, and he was thrilled at our creativity.

I found out years later that he had passed away from a heart attack on his way to a big race in Northridge, California in 2002). It was very sad when I heard. He had always treated me like everyone else in the office, even though I was only 18 years old and not nearly as hip as the rest. I really had no songwriting experience.

As far as Phil went, I knew of Ronnie, Darlene, Tina Turner, and so forth, but was so green. In fact, I'm sure that, eventually, many came around to visit Marshall ... Annette, Snuff, Donnie, Lou Adler and others. They all loved him. He was a big part of the Hollywood music biz behind the scenes. He always had a smile for me and everyone else.

Rockin' Nam

To this day, I could kick myself that I wasn't more tuned in. I'm forever saddened I didn't pay more attention to chat with them. How I could have learned so much about the valuable experiences they all went through. I'm very frustrated about that to this day. I loved going to the office every morning. Not one to get up early, this was a life-changing period for me. Everything I was into now was different.

Weekday mornings, I'd show up at 9 a.m., and the vibe couldn't have been better. The secretary's name was Muriel. She was so kind and loved everyone's energy. She made everything ten times nicer. Muriel would type up song lyrics anytime we asked. She was always so interested in what we were doing. If she didn't have time, she *made* time. It seems like Muriel was my biggest fan.

From Brentwood, it was a beautiful drive to Hollywood, down Sunset, through Beverly Hills, past Doheny, then to the right and past Schwab's, and into the complex on the left at 8983. The other half of the duplex was occupied by Jim and Bob Webb. Of course, today everyone knows what a songwriter Jimmy Webb is—and a nice guy too. Now and then, I would wander over to the Webb office and chat with him for a few minutes (very cool). In retrospect, Jim Webb was a very busy guy and for him to take time out to give some teenage kid attention.

We'd put songs together every day. Writers came in with their lyrics, scribbled out on a piece of paper, and we'd come up with the right tune. At the end of the day, we'd lay them down on a small tape player, (one of those old Craig recorders with the gear shift).

SIDENOTE: I had no idea what kind of talent I was dealing with, but one thing was for sure, there were some heavy hitters in there. I can't be specific but I saw several dignitaries walk in and out of there.

One day a very tall Black man walked in. He was about six foot seven and very fun. He had a smile that would light up the world. His name was Freeman King. He had these great big teeth and a smile that lit it up. Few recognized it back then, but Freeman was a multi-talented actor-writer-performer. Among other things, he would go on to be a cast member on *The Sonny & Cher Show*. Later, he would portray the emcee in the film, *The Buddy Holly Story*, cutting up and making announcements center stage at the Apollo.

Through the years, he was very active in many other ventures such as film, TV, and commercials. Everyone loved this guy, and he knew *EVERYBODY*! He and I had a great camaraderie. He was the first guy I ever met that voiced the philosophy that you should have a "day job." He drove for Western Union during the day and pursued his career in between. Freeman lived on Sweetzer Avenue, just minutes from the Holloway dr. where actor, Sal Mineo resided and was unfortunately was killed in 1976, a sad story indeed. Some years later, I would meet up with Freeman's good friend, Murray Langston (the Unknown Comic) while taping a few *Gong Shows*. (I did five of them.) Murray had stories about Freeman. He said they had a ball cruising around together making connections. He told me that he and Freeman were always sharing information. They'd often hang.

JULY – 1969

In '69, Freeman and I went to work on a song of his called "Mr. & Mrs. Jones" (not the Billy Paul tune). It was a lot of fun, and interesting enough, this kind of thing came very natural to me. A few years later, the song was published under both our names in a catalogue.

One night, Freeman called me up (at 7:30 p.m. or so). I remember him calling once,

"I need you to come down ... to back me up on my set ... at the club."

"Where *are* you," I asked.

"The Redd Foxx Club on La Brea," he said.

(I'd seen the club while driving around).

"Freeman," I reminded him. "I'm only eighteen."

"That's OK," he assured me, "just come to the side door."

What would happen if they caught me underage? I worried that he might push too far and possibly do damage to his career, a career that he'd worked so hard to build up.

"I just don't want to get you in any trouble."
He'd just laugh out loud and say,

"Don't be so uptight, man ... everything's cool," and then he'd laugh a big hearty laugh.

He was such a celebrity, they tended to really let him slide. Following his instructions, I drove down to Sunset and turned right on La Brea. I slid in the side door. I backed him up on two numbers (one of them, was the new tune we wrote). The crowd loved it. I was proud ... happy for him. Later, however, time went by, and we drifted apart—especially when I left town.

Rockin' Nam

Sadly, we fell out of touch. Hey, it happens. LA, at the time, was ripe with that, "here-today-gone-tomorrow" lifestyle of the '70s. On a winter day in 1999, Murray gave me a phone number. I was able to talk to Freeman on the phone. We had such a great chat about the past and the present. He got a huge kick out of the fact that I'd been playing blues and doing stand-up. Little did I know, but that would be the last time I'd ever speak with Freeman King again. He died shortly after that phone call.

So, with a tear in my eye, I am forever grateful that I caught up with Freeman King before he passed and had the chance to share thoughts and laughs with him before it was too late. Murray and I continue to chat a lot about Freeman now and then. I will be forever grateful for that experience I had at the publishing company and all those memories. It was a fortunate break to wind up in that position at such a young age. As for the song ("Mrs. Jones"), it seems a production company has used it. It's been in some projects (some films and other things). I was shocked that it even made its way around town.

In 1978, I got a letter from Beachwood Music. The letter stated that I was the co-author, and it was housed in their offices off Gower Street. Somewhere around 2007, I would receive a check from EMI for the use of the song. I don't know when or how he added me to the publishing, but I'm so grateful. And the money was so timely. Just when I was down to "rock bottom" (again), I get this nice check. It's hard to forget those great days at 8983 Sunset—the song, Marshal, Freeman, Muriel ... the people I worked with, those who came by, all of it.

Rockin' Nam

It was just plain and simple, the greatest time in my young life, not to mention, the greatest time in "the business" … The writing, the lifestyle, everything — simply unforgettable. Years later, I would brag to my friends,

"Hey, I played the REDD FOXX club!

SEX DRUGS & ROCK N' ROLL
6.

January - 1971

A few days passed as I hung around the motor pool, gassing up trucks, and already growing impatient. At dusk, we were all on the roof (our usual sundown gathering). A guy traveling through, looking very worn, wanders over and starts telling us a story that really made us think twice about our "roaming habits." I felt especially guilty because I was no saint. I just had to sit and listen. The guy was almost in tears, and everyone sat up and took notice. He proceeded to tell the story. Apparently, one of his close buds met an ugly death while roaming around (like I just did). The story involved information about a NEW situation that was happening more and more around 'Nam.

So now what? Now, the enemy had gotten involved sexually? They had started to go beyond ruthless and got into morbid. We took this guy seriously; he'd been in-country longer than any of us. He informed us that the enemy (VC), was lurking around in very sick and perverse ways. He was serious as we all pulled our chairs in. Listening close now, what I heard next rocked me (and a lot of others) to their core. It was chilling. He told us that his best friend and homey, Marty, who he had known since they were eleven, had always been a major "poon-hound," and once he got to the 'Nam, he was in heaven. "Girls were everywhere," he explained.

125

"However, since the army got stricter, it became harder and harder to go into the Ville and now he was out of patience. Marty was always lamenting that he really missed the old days when we had so much freedom to come and go."

Now the guy was getting very emotional, and the more he talked, the weaker his voice would get. It was very effective, and we all started listening with great immediacy. He said his friend had a big problem getting out—getting girls.

"They won't let me go nowhere, he'd always say. He tried to sneak out a few times but they'd always catch him. One night, he finally got out. That's the last time we ever saw him," the guy said with a tear in his eye.

As the story goes and from the info they had, he went to the Ville to get laid but was having no luck. Instead of coming back, he proceeded to go further into the village. He finally found some "skank" who would do him for cheap. They don't know exactly where he was, but it wasn't good. The guy teared up again and said that they tried to talk to him and warn him that he wasn't in Kansas anymore. They warned him that things could get weird, could be dangerous.

"We *ARE* in a war zone, ya know."

"I know, I know," he'd always say.

"Well," (wiping his face), "they found him three days later in an empty farmhouse face down in a pool of blood."

"What the fuck?" I said. "What happened?" (I'm not sure I wanted to hear the answer. It can't be good).

The guy continued...

126

Rockin' Nam

"Well, it seems he met up with a woman, alright. Only apparently, she was VC (Viet Cong), and it seemed she DID him all right. She must have been very cruel because what she did to him..."

Now he breaks down...sobbing. We all looked at each other in horror. It was reported that she had gone and inserted a piece of cork up inside her vagina.

SIDENOTE: The cork had several razor blades pushed into it and protruding out. Therefore, upon insertion, the harder and deeper a guy would go, well, you get the idea.

Barely able to speak now, he said,
"He sliced himself up. I don't think he had any idea what he was getting himself into. He was just young, dumb, and desperate. He was naive, unaware, inexperienced, and unprepared."

At this point the guy was a mess. He told us that the villagers remembered hearing shrill screams in the night, but they didn't know what to make of it. The guy was losing it, voice trembling and shaking horribly, he continued,

"Fact is, he didn't even realize what was happening until he was done ... Word was that he felt light-headed as he pulled out of her. He rolled over and passed out. She just left him there, dying in a pool of his own semen and blood."

(Dude was in tears).

I was in shock. I couldn't believe what this guy was telling us. What the F**k? My friends and I tried to console him, tell him that we'd take his story to heart and watch ourselves, but it didn't help much. His friend had gone through things no one could imagine. It was very, very difficult for this guy to retell the story and relay it to us.

He did, however, get his point across!

I vowed to be cool. I'd never heard a story like this. It scared the shit out of me. I had trouble sleeping for a few nights. It was hard getting those pictures out of my mind. They were pretty haunting. We were starting to get more info on this conflict. I was shocked by the story, really shaken. What a *MIND FUCK!!!*

I tried not to freak, but I was pretty rattled. Deep down inside, I was trying to make myself a vow to keep the sex to a minimum and stay out the way of disasters like this one

… GOOD LUCK WITH THAT!

Man, as if it was bad enough to even be *in* "NAM!" then there this kind of nastiness. What's a guy supposed to do—give it up? I'd just have to be extra careful. I'd just have to check and double check now. If it looks weird and strange, it probably is. It would probably be smart to keep away from those backwoods also …

NO MORE STRAYING!

I may have been a cherry in-country, but I was learning fast. Glad we got the "heads up" on this one, even though it was ugly. It was important to hear before I even had a chance to think about getting in trouble.

Rockin' Nam

Later, I received some great news. It was the mail I was waiting for, and I didn't quite realize it then, but it was going to change my life! I was about to embark on the journey of a lifetime! Finally, I got my orders!

THE BIG TOUR!

The next day I walked around in a daze. It was like a dream—orders from the big city! It was another chance to get with a band and do what I always wanted to do … ROCK! A couple of days passed and it was getaway day. I headed to Saigon! I did say goodbye and thanked all the guys as I was to catch a lift.

As I rode the convoy down south, I thought, I'm getting another chance! I thought of the big audition. I *HAD* to get this gig! My whole life right now depended on getting this gig. I couldn't believe Cap let me go. What was it like down there in the big city?" "Who will I meet?"

We rode along; all of us in one truck. I had a guitar in one hand and duffle bag in the other. I looked around at everyone holding their M-16s. I slowly pushed the six-string between my bag and the seat—to hide it. I sat back and read the *Stars and Stripes*. I thought back to the early days in Cam Ranh, with the first band. I thought about our old "crib," all decked out with a hammock, black light, posters, a cool stereo playing one of my only two albums over and over. I reminisced about Kim, our housekeeper. I remember asking her what her name was.

"Keeem," she said softly.

Of course, that was *Kim*, in my vocabulary. I watched as she hung clothes outside (she did laundry). When she came around, I always had a big smile on my face, lots of chemistry between the two of us—very sensual. It lasted the duration of the time I spent in Cam Ranh. I wasn't sure if she understood who I was or what I did exactly, but one thing is for sure, we really *did* get along nicely. I think I taught her a lot—and vise-verse. I recall looking out at her and being sad that she had to collect dirty laundry every day and hang the wet clothes on the line to dry. She wasn't necessarily "school" educated, but she was street wise. Sometimes I thought,

"What if we got together?"

Oh well. In the end, I'd probably let her down. I was too young to think about any kind of a real relationship, especially ten thousand miles away. I was all of eighteen! Besides, I had a career, a music career.

Sadly, when I left Cam Ranh for Don Zoom, I was so fucked up that I never said goodbye. In fact, I never even TRIED to look anyone up. I just pouted, felt sorry for myself, and split. I often wondered,

"How did she turn out? Where is she today?"

Why didn't I go out of my way to stop in and see her? …as much traveling as I did?

Suddenly I opened my eyes! As I awoke, there was some commotion that jarred me. Apparently, there was some activity in the area. No one knew *what* it was or *where* it was. The convoy commander ordered everyone out of the trucks and into to foxholes along the side of the road. The shout of "smoke 'em if you got 'em" went out. Some of us heard strange noises, but it didn't amount to much of anything, still I found myself in the foxhole, next to a bunch of guys while they waited to see what was going to happen.

Rockin' Nam

I looked at the guy on my right …and then I looked to the guy on my left. We stared at each other and while *they* were equipped with their backpacks and M-16s, they noticed that I was in the foxhole with my guitar. What a picture *this* was. All the GIs in the convoy had their gear on with rifles slung over their shoulders … and there I was … with my guitar. Can you just imagine that? I must have looked so out of place as I sat with all of them. I know I wasn't in the same "mind-set" as they were, but I also didn't want to feel like a weirdo. I was trying my best to be cool and just blend in. This dude started fuckin' with me. He spoke up,

"Who you going to hurt with that thing?" (lots of laughter all around!)

Acting a little oversensitive (it hit a nerve), I felt compelled to lash out …

"Oh, I don't know, I snapped back, "Maybe your mom? … breaking into my hooch? … at midnight … in a camouflage teddy?" (lots of cackling).
The guy was stunned. He didn't know whether to laugh or kick my ass. He was a little surprised that this was coming out of the mouth of such a young punk. The others were bent over with laughter, which made it worse between this guy and me. I recognized the guy's ire so I tried to lighten up the vibe. I felt I had to square it away with the guy.

"Hey, my guitar is the only thing I'm comfortable with."

The guy mellowed a bit with a half a smile and mumbled something, but I couldn't make it out. I felt bad, but I just couldn't let the comment go unnoticed.

Rockin' Nam

The activity passed, and we were getting closer to the big city. I was headed for the entertainment building. I got dropped off a few blocks from the SSVN (Special Services Viet Nam) building. I walked over. It was around 3:00 or 3:30 p.m. I went inside and looked for a person in charge. A very attractive girl named Linn pointed me the right direction. She was very pretty and had a great smile. We all would wind up flirting with her constantly.

I found my way to the right department. I had my lucky jacket on (the one with the California flag sewn on the back) funky fatigue pants, sand-blown army boots and wore my usual lot of bracelets and beads (acquired from the Montegnard kids). Suddenly a short man came out in a perfectly pressed army uniform. He guessed that I was there to see him.

"Are you PFC. Flynn?" he asked.

"Ah, yes, I am," I said.

"OK, c'mon back."

I followed the guy down a long narrow hallway and into a back office. The building smelled musty. It was similar to places in my past. Places with structures like the club house at Malibu Lake or some hotels I'd been in. You can always smell that aura. It takes me back decades to the past. It paints a picture of what times were like back then. It's eerie, but every time I smell that distinct smell, I get the same feeling … brings me back to my younger days. It was kind of an "I'd been here before" feeling.

All of a sudden, this guy plops himself down behind a desk and started in. He interviewed me and then asked me to play a little guitar … so I did.

He wasn't that impressed. I told him that I was raring to go, that I was looking forward to getting rehearsed and out on the road. He still didn't warm but instead continued explaining how the operation worked. He collected names and numbers and filed them all inside of a rolodex he kept on his desk. I felt like I was getting nowhere. I really didn't want to, but reluctantly, I decided to reconstruct the "BIG LIE."

"Well, I don't know if you were aware of this, but I used to play with Grand Funk," I boasted — again.

He just sat there with no reaction. It was like he was too preoccupied to hear what I had to say. I'm thinking,

"Who the fuck is this guy anyway?

Suddenly, he bellows out,

"Great! A couple of the guys I sent out last week, played with Curtis Mayfield … and a few weeks back.

"I sent a guy out that spent some time with Spencer Davis."

"We got lots of guys from lots of bands."

I started to feel sick. I was in over my head. I was down in the big city "giggin' with the heavies. Of course, I now realized that I was just a "number" in a sea of great talent *AND*, interviewing with a guy that didn't really dig my scene, a guy who probably abhorred hippie freaks like me. After all, it *was* still the ARMY! Apparently, he had a collection of guys he wanted and bands he put together. I didn't fit in. I wasn't his type. I was just too much of a "freak" for him. Soon, he verified it when he closed of the interview. Then he said,

"Well, I've got your information."

"I appreciate you coming down here. I've got a few more auditions today."

I was really bummin' as he said,

"Well, we'll input you in the rolodex, and if we need you, we'll let you know. Thanks for stopping by." OK, now I *am* sick, sick as a dog. I was freakin'. I turned white. I thought I was going to faint. Of all the guys to run into in this city, at this audition, in this situation, it has to be this guy?

I said my "thank-yous" (very weakly) and slowly walked away. I went toward the door and out the walkway. A million thoughts were in my head and nothing good. How could this be? How could this happen to me? And why?

I slowly made my way through the door and onto the outside walkway past a line of offices that led to the street. With my head down, I don't think I could have gotten any lower. I kept asking myself, "Why? How could I possibly return to my unit empty-handed? Does this mean I'm not gonna play another gig in 'Nam?

"How can go back, as a failure, and play army?" I kept hearing Cap's voice in my head...

"And don't come back without that gig."

Dejected as hell, I ambled down the walkway; I was very tired and very depressed. I was almost too weak and depressed to walk. I tried to make my way out of the complex to the street. All of a sudden, I hear something. For a minute, I thought I was hallucinating, but, from the very last office, I *did* hear a whisper ... "Psssst." A voice was trying to summon me from across the way. I heard it! It came out of the darkness from the very last office, a small dark nook that was hard to see. I cautiously approached the door. It was slightly ajar. It was dark and kind of spooky in there. A guy appeared.

"Hey, I'm Doug. I fix stuff ... guitars, amps, whatever ... I play bass too..."

"Cool. I'm Flyn."

"You used to play with Grand Funk? That is *SO* hip," he said acting surprised and really impressed.

"Yes," I said sheepishly, trying to change the subject soon as possible, "I'm pretty bummed right now. I had everything riding on this gig ... and to make matters worse, the guy wasn't into me at all."

"Oh, don't worry about him," Doug assured me.

"I can fix it so you're down here soon!"

"WHAT? No way!" I said shockingly.

"I'll just take your card from the rolodex and move it to the front of the line." He explained.

"Oh my God! If you could do that, I would owe you big time." I begged.

"Hey, no prob'," he said nonchalantly.

"It's the least I can do for a talented bro like you."

I was blown away. What a shocker. Imagine this guy bailing me out like this, with the gig of a lifetime. Then he says,

"What are you doing tonight?"

"Nothing" I answered.

"Come by about 10 p.m." he suggested.

"Ok," I said.

I was thinking to myself ...

"What a break! Who *is* this guy? How great was it to meet him? What if he would have been away from his office for a minute. I would have never met him! As the sun went down, I wandered around in a daze. I didn't know what was to happen at 10 o'clock, but I was excited. I could still hear Cap's voice …

"Better get that gig, son. Don't come back here empty-handed."

Well, if Doug was sincere (and I think he was), it looked like I might be rockin' soon—amazing! There were thoughts racing through my head at a rapid pace: Who's the band? Where will we rehearse? Who will I get matched with? I felt some angst coming on. I had a number of emotions going through my head. After all, it had been a hell of a trip from Don Zoom to Saigon … so much action in such a small amount of time. From Cap letting me go on the trip, to little "Napoleon" turning me down—*and now*— possible salvation, thanks to Doug.

I got to the building at 10 p.m. Doug had a lot of equipment set up to jam. There were keyboards, amps, and gear everywhere. I walked in with a smile on my face. Doug greeted me with open arms. He told me that we were going to jam. He also told me to go over to the long, wooden closet and open it up to pick out a guitar. I walked over and opened the huge fake oak slider and ...

There must have been twenty or twenty-five Gibson guitars: SGs, Flying Vs, 335s, Firebirds— incredible. I picked out a 1969, sunburst Firebird. The amps were also Gibson. Not great, but it was obvious that the Army had an endorsement with Gibson the gear. All of this was shocking to me. I never dreamed I'd see all this cool gear.

Rockin' Nam

Imagine all this right here in the middle of a conflict—thousands and thousands of miles away.

I gazed out upon this huge room we were gathered in. There were a couple of keyboards set up. There was also a big bass amp and a bass guitar as well as an adequate P.A. system. All good stuff! Set up for what? Were we going to have the "jam of the century?" Right on cue, another guy came waltzing in. He was very hip-looking …Had a huge, well-trimmed mustache. He looked very cool. He carried himself well. He approaches … big hugs all around.

Doug announces,

"Flyn, this is Stoney, the best keyboard player around."

We shook hands. There were smiles everywhere. Stoney remarked,

"Just got the word. Doug invited… here we are."

"Well, Doug is very cool, isn't he?" I added.

"AMEN!" said Stoney.

"Good to meet you," I said.

We found out, as we jammed, that Doug was a fan of the progressive bands—bands like, Gentle Giant, Emerson Lake & Palmer, and especially, the band "Yes." Stoney, on the other hand was classically trained. He had gone to college and was playing Mozart and Chopin since he was 8. He also dug the bands of the day. And then there was myself?

I was the Buffalo Springfield, CSN, Poco type—lot of acoustic music ... Stills, Young, Paul Simon, etc. I was a big fan of the "acoustic" music. I'd played electric but since I fell in with the coffee house crowd, I tended to lean towards acoustic stuff.

Rockin' Nam

We started jamming around eleven, and by twelve, we were really *gelling* and having fun. By 12:30, the girls came by. Shit! Groupies! They were cute, hip, and digging the music. They wore jeans and Ts—*very* hip! The girls made us play better as we started to show off. We didn't take a break! We played until about 2:30. I put the Gibson Firebird down and hugged the guys.

We made big plans. We all vowed to get together and reconnect back in the world. The chemistry between us was really great and we had a ball being on the same page musically.

After the marathon jam, I sashayed over to the girls. They were so cool and in a hip style. They asked some really great questions about songs, bands, America, and so forth. It was such a joy talking to them. We chatted for a few minutes. I gravitated to the cutest one … we smiled at each other and had some small talk for a few minutes. I posed the question…

"It's getting late. Do you know any motels around here?"

She got a combination of looks on her face and grabbed my hand and said,

"Don't be a goof, man, you're coming with me."

"What's your name," I asked.

"Nikki," she said.

Ah, the life of a guitar player … always the girl.

We all said goodbye, and I thanked Doug over and over. I told Stoney that I'd see him soon. We all agreed on how natural it came together and how great it would be if we ever had any real time to make it work. We all agreed and praised each other for being the hippest guys in 'Nam. Doug was a genius on the bass.

Rockin' Nam

Stoney was nothing but awesome on keyboards. What a pleasure, to be jamming with these guys. I could have gone all night. We swore to get together soon. We bonded nicely and it was a no-brainer to do it again. We promised. However, it would be quite a long time before we reconnected and it wouldn't be in "Nam."

SIDENOTE: Actually, we never *DID* jam again, (in 'Nam, that is). It wasn't until I got home; I made my way down south. Can you believe it? I actually made my way back to Louisiana ... AGAIN! I looked them up, and we put a group together! We wound up touring Lafayette, New Orleans, Houston, and Austin, and we had some success. What can I say? I got incredibly lucky. I was with some talented guys!

I walked on and over to my date and said,
"OK, I think I'm ready now."
She smiled back, took my arm and said,
"I'm ready too."
"What an unexpected pleasure," I thought.
We headed for her place. I was thinking what a fantastic life I was living ... the band in Cam Ranh, Don Zume, now apparently a second tour—in Saigon, a jam with the guys, and now I'm on my way home with Nikki. Just then, we heard a huge explosion in the distance. I flinched for a second as she clutched my arm. We walked down streets of blackness, very late on an eerie Saigon evening. What a picture. There we were, her arm entangled in mine (kind of like that Dylan album cover with Suze Rotolo).

Rockin' Nam

We got to her place. It was great! So here she is, thousands of miles across the Pacific, eighteen years old, and she's got her own place, her own life, and her own job. I was proud of her. We played around for a while and then she said,

"Time for sleep now … gotta get up for work in a few hours. Go ahead, let yourself out in the morning."

I cuddled up with her and said, "OK."
"What a great time," I whispered.

"Yes!" she said.

She wrapped herself around me (spooning) and said,

"I completely agree."

In the blink of an eye, the alarm was blaring. She was up. I tried to figure out where I was … how did I get there?

I tried to get my bearings. How can she get up? She was putting her makeup on. She looked so cute. I watched her in the mirror. I couldn't take my blurry eyes off her. She was even prettier than the night before. In another situation, I could have just stayed there … indefinitely! She smiled at me.

"Great night," I muttered.

"Yes. It was, "she echoed. "You guys sounded so good... it was great. You guys should play together. Too bad they can't send YOU all out to tour ... that would be a special group."

I NEVER SAW HER AGAIN!

Later that morning (after sleeping in), I got up and went out on the town. I didn't know what to do or where to go, but I wasn't too worried about it.

Rockin' Nam

I decided to cruise around the city, maybe do some sightseeing. I had a little breakfast somewhere, and then I decided to get a pedi-cab. The driver was interesting. He started weaving in and out of traffic. As we sped through the middle of town Saigon, there I was, sitting in a scoop, on the front of some motor vehicle driven by this Vietnamese crazy man.

The guy was a combination of Evel Knievel and Mr. Magoo. No Shit! We began to soar through the city, it was amazing. Everything was so colorful. We drove past the golf course, the grass was soooo *GREEN*. I just stared, and then I smiled and eventually started to laugh. The driver was laughing too. He was laughing because I was laughing. It was bizarre. We must have driven around for hours … well at least, for forty-five minutes.

We stopped in a pretty mellow part of town, and I was hyper. I was ready to party. I went into a couple of bars. There were some bands, Filipino, I think. Some girls came over, but they weren't that attractive. In fact, they were pretty funky, to be honest. I didn't know what I was looking for, but after spending some time in the city, I mellowed a bit. I felt like walking. I went in and out of several bars. I lot all track of time. By now, it was getting into evening. I wandered into a fairly low-end part of town. As I walked on, I had a serious talk with myself.

"You're an idiot … what's wrong with you? Who does this? Who walks around a foreign country at all hours with such disregard?"

I was really gambling now. I walked down the road on a warm, dark, ominous, uncertain evening. I can't remember where I spent the night, but I woke up in one piece. I forgot how I got there but got up and headed down the road. I did, *however,* have the wherewithal to recognize that I was far outside of the city limits … probably in another village. I could have gotten so messed up. As security strengthened in the 'Nam, I came up with new and different ways of keeping my lifestyle going.

Since I was "Mr. Rock 'n' Roll," I had some extra leeway. However, all that would be tested in the days to come. I was enjoying my day off. I was wandering—all of a sudden—I get stopped by the MPs. Apparently, they were caught up with my dressing habits, as well as my manner and style. You could tell that the situation in "Nam" was getting pretty weird when you had MPs wandering around checking for uniform violations. I was just being "me" and didn't really give a "rat's ass" what anybody thought. I guess I was looking pretty funky, sloppy, very 60's California "hippie-ish"… no military-like at all. I had the "Cali" flag sewn on the back of my fatigue jacket. I had the name "Stills" (as in Stephen Stills) stitched into my hat. I had beads and bracelets all over myself. I also had a small, custom-made, gold peace sign around my neck … I watched them as they made their way toward me.
"ARE YOU KIDDIN' ME? THE FASHION POLICE?!"

They stopped and detained me for an hour, and I discovered that something brand-new had begun. They had started a new procedure of taking pictures (for proof) and writing GIs up for various acts of breaking army codes. They would nab different perpetrators of different protocol, including breaking dress codes, wearing wild hats, and other bullshit. Instead of any kind of punishment right there on the scene—like being written up—they'd snap a photo and send it back to your CO and/or various authorities.

I, being my cynical self, asked if I could pose any way I saw fit. They calmly answered,

"Sure."

I was, having pics taken while giving them the middle finger, (flipping them off!) I was acting crazy. I was cackling with delight while the MPs went through everything. I had gotten to Nam innocently enough but now, my demeanor was changing! I made some snide comments. They just ignored me and drove on.

I finally made my way back to Don Zume, and after being back a short time, I felt comfortable. These guys were, without a doubt, the coolest dudes on the planet. I was so proud to be part of the 577th. On my first night back, I was looking forward to hanging out.

I wanted to bond with my guys again. I wanted to swap stories, while I rested up and waited for orders that were to come from Saigon. Thanks to my new friend Doug, I told the guys, I couldn't wait to get down there and …

"Rock the world!

Rockin' Nam

SAIGON
7.

The CO out at the 577th was very similar to Cap in Cam Ranh. He got a kick out of me, but he didn't want me pushing the envelope … he didn't want me calling the shots. After roaming around for a week or so, I was a nervous wreck. I was trying so hard to quell my anticipation and trying not to drive myself crazy. Finally, after a couple weeks, the orders arrived. Even *I* was shocked when they came in. *WOW*—he did it! He actually did it! That fucker came through for me! How cool was this! It was almost too good to be true! Orders came from Saigon, and you just knew that my CO would start messing with me.

"I don't know if I should let you go to this 'gig' of yours," he blurted out.

"Are you kidding me, Cap … I was born to rock," I said with a smile.

The CO messes with me a little more…

He dishes it out,

"Who's going to take your place? Who's gonna pump my gas?"

"Oh, you got lots of guys," (mess with him back).

"Besides, what about my rock 'n' roll career?"

Rockin' Nam

After pausing for an extended period of time, the captain, of course, had to harass me one more time.

"Listen, Private! What about my motor pool?"

"You can handle it, Cap," I said.

And just to mess with him a little more, I started singing…

"*Get your motor-pool running…*" (ala Steppenwolf)

"Now that's funny," Cap says, smiling big.

"All I have to say is; you better go kick some ass (he breaks a half a smile).

"Oh, you can count on it, Sir," I assured him.

SIDENOTE: I'll never forget how excited I was when he let me go. I was ready for Saigon, to meet the band, to see my new friend Doug and to tour again. I was giddy. This was going to be epic! HEY, the first tour (out of the 35th in Cam Ranh) was great, but it was small. This was "the real deal"… the "Big One." It was to be a world tour of every village in 'Nam, with talented musicians, rehearsal spaces, itineraries, and more—YES!

I made my way down south, and of course, I had to go see Doug. I was like a kid in a candy store and with a big man-hug; I told him how much I appreciated everything. I told him that I couldn't believe he came through for me. He said he needed to get me out there.

"I need you to go out to rock the troops; they'll really dig you … You're too good NOT to be touring," he said.

Rockin' Nam

I couldn't believe what I was hearing — especially after that ugly breakup in Cam Ranh. What a difference a few weeks make. The next morning, we gathered in a rehearsal hall at the complex. I met the new band. There was a whole group of very talented cats. As usual, I took the lead and sketched out a cool song list. I always made sure that we played some different stuff—cool stuff, not-too-commercial stuff. I always threw in a few surprises.

The next day, we got our itinerary. It looked good. We were to travel the entire country of South Vietnam, top to bottom. This was going to be epic! A few days later, I put in a special request and asked that Don Zume be put on the schedule. I wanted to play for my buddies at the 577th. In a couple of days, my request to add Don Zume was approved.

What they usually did was give the band a week to rehearse, and then off we'd go. It was a ball—no snags, no problems. We were about to head out to a great adventure. I felt great! Things were really happening.

The first gig was near a town called Phan Thiet. The memories were a little hazy, but whatever it was, it was pretty good. The band was a little rough because of being new and all, but we came together quickly, and it was great! It was going to be a blast! As we continued on to Nha Trang, Qui Nhon, An Khe, up to Quang Tri, and eventually Da Nang, Hue, and Dong Ha.

We were officially ROCKERS in the "Nam."

Every day, we'd wake up and get some juice or coffee. We'd cruise around and often talk about the last gig, and then we were on to the next gig.

It hardly felt like we were even in the Army!

Rockin' Nam

One thing that was important was the fact that we didn't walk around with a "tude" or any "airs." Because of that, we were always well received. Unfortunately, I started doing a little more partying, and that *WASN'T* good. The band ignored it for the most part, although,

A few days into the tour, we were brought to a prison camp, somewhere near Pleiku, I think. It was a facility where the US was holding the enemy. They warned us not to take any pictures (although I think someone did). In fact, this gig was just thrown in at the last minute.

We set up, and the prisoners began to gather. Wow! I was looking around at Viet Cong, Red Chinese, North Vietnamese, little kids—like nine-year-old boys and girls—also, teenage boys.

How in the world was *THIS* happening? ... I was amazed! I was learning something new every day, I really was. I would have never known about this gig if I hadn't got into this CMTS (Command Military Touring Shows) thing. We were guessing that the army was trying to give them a break—a diversion.

Anyway, we got started, and the roomful of prisoners seemed to like it. They were bopping to the music and nodding their heads. I was pretty sure they had no idea what the band was singing, but on a certain level, music is fairly universal.

We did the set, got some applause, and got out of there. I heard rumors that some the guys snuck a couple of pics, but never saw them. I was such a trip to play for prisoners. I'm not sure anyone else ever did that. I can't think of any.

Rockin' Nam

The next night we played another Army base, Kon Tum. The show was great. I got with a bunch of GIs after the show. They were so cool and complimentary. They told me how much they appreciated us coming all the way out, and that they dug how much the band took the gig seriously—how we worked our asses off to rock. Some of them told us that they'd been out in the middle of nowhere for so long that they almost forgot what good music sounded like. They just couldn't believe it when we showed up.

"Man, you guys were great. Your version of 'Roadhouse Blues' was the best," one guy said.

"Thanks for the kind words … we appreciate you guys and are happy to come out," I told them.

"We thought you were going to be just another bullshit band playing the same old crap," another remarked. I smiled real big.

THAT MEANT *EVERYTHING* TO ME!

As the night wore on, we were chitchatting about just about everything under the sun. I wound up on some kind of stacked-up sand bag listening to this some great music. I loved those moments.

Soon, a bleach-blond, weathered-looking, E-4 (Army specialist) was telling some chilling stories.

Don't know if he was bullshitting us or what but we listened. He told us how he'd been in-country for more than three years and that he kept re-upping to stay over. He explained that he'd gotten used to the lifestyle, that he had no real "life" back in the world. He said his wife left him during his first go-round. She split with some guy from the neighborhood who dodged the draft. He admitted that he tried to commit suicide a few times.

"Luckily, this nice Vietnamese young lady took me in and gave me TLC 'till I got better ... now I'm good."

He stated that he got so used to "the Nam," he didn't want to go back. He didn't want to be anywhere else. Everyone was fascinated. He went on to say that he'd been shot a few times, and that once he was in a chopper and the enemy shot it down. He was hit and jumped out of the vehicle. He landed in a tree. The enemy moved in, and the guys on the ground were helpless. However, he was in perfect position in the trees and had a great angle and position to fire on the enemy. He could hit them without knowing where it was coming from. He got most of them and saved his group.

"Really?" someone asked.

He then proceeded to say that he was with "Charlie" company in the middle of nowhere during the infamous TET of '68.

"No way," someone shot back.

"It was the weirdest scene ever," he said.

"We were walking through this tiny village. There were a bunch of kids playing outside, and all of a sudden—one by one—guys around me were getting hit and we finally figured that there really evil and sly."

"There were shooters inside the house. They were hiding amongst the families, using them as shields. They picked us off one at a time. The lieutenant told us to get down and that we should get out of there."

He continued...

"We didn't want to hurt the kids. It was a difficult situation but he end came when this little girl came out with a loaf of bread ... came out of the thatched roof abode. She walked all the way out to the road and offered it up to one of the guys. (Now he started to tear up. Talk about feeling uncomfortable; we lowered our heads.) The little girl handed it to Smitty, (pause) and then she ran away; (pause) … it blew up in his face, killing him and two guys around him."

He explained that it was then the officer gave the order to wipe out everything.

"It was ugly. It's a memory I'll never get out of my head … but we got rid of all those fuckers," he sighed.

He added that he thought the lieutenant was summoned back to D.C. and given a court marshal for the action. This was very eerie.

"You all right?" I asked.

"As good as can be, things considered," he said.

Later, we were guessing that it was My Lai he was referring to, and the lieutenant was Calley.

The things he said could never be substantiated. I had no idea what time it was. It didn't really matter anyway. Who was going to keep track? It was "the Nam;" it was the "after-gig" party! I was living large — and playing music for the guys!

The next day, I dragged my ass up, and we headed for Da Nang. I didn't know it yet, but the tour was about to get even better. We had the day off and camped somewhere. I went into the Ville and found some girls and we partied a little. I was apparently oblivious to any kind of danger. I don't think I really knew where the guys went. The band rarely hung out together and I don't remember partying together.

Rockin' Nam

The following day, we headed out. We were up and at 'em ... off to the officers' club located at China Beach in Da Nang. We'd heard of this place. It was one of the only "mini-R & R" spots *in-country*. If a GI didn't want to leave the country, he could lay out at China Beach for three days. We took off. It was another chopper ride, and guess who I ran into—again?

AMY was on board! I couldn't help but flirt.

"We've got to stop meeting like this, Amy."

"I know ... people are beginning to talk," she playfully retorted.

Oh man, this is why I was growing so fond of her. She always said the perfect thing, the hip thing—the best thing. I was sleepy and wanted to nod out, but I would always get befuddled around her. She was so cool and good looking. I really had a thing for her. I only wished that this was under different circumstances. I would have so loved to have met up with a quality person like this back home.

She was just the kind of girl with qualities I often looked for. Back in the day, the kids were getting' wild but there were still some that had it "together"...that's the girl I was always looking for, someone I could trust and believe in.

The officers' club here was similar to the one in Cam Ranh, except it was bigger and seemed to be a little swankier. This was *THEEE* vacation spot for those who wanted to relax *"IN-COUNTRY."* It was an R & R locale for soldiers and officers who couldn't leave town. So there I am, backstage, about to go on and after smoking a joint, I was ready for the show. I'd never been shy about getting high or getting wild, especially before a gig.

Rockin' Nam

The familiar sound of M-16s and mortars nearby provided an eerie audible backdrop. The band was waiting in the green room (the kitchen) ready to go on and do a huge concert for the troops at the club at China Beach. Unbelievably, the crowd was chanting the band's name over and over in anticipation. We were ready to rock! I was impressed that our reputation had preceded us and that ABC News had showed up in Da Nang to set up lights and cameras for a taping. It appeared that our band was getting some major recognition.

"Wow," said Booker (the bass player),

"How cool is this?"

Arizona (trumpet and rhythm guitar) threw in,

"Man, we better be good."

At that moment (almost on cue), a very hip-guy in his 30's walked up and introduced himself —

"Hey," he said.

" Steve Bell, ABC News ... how are you?"

"Good, I answered. What's going on?"

"Well, we heard that *you* were the "guys!""

"We're going to put a couple cameras on you, film you, and maybe do a story."

"Wow, that would be so cool," I said.

"Amen!" said a kid hanging around.

Since we were so popular and since there were a lot of GIs suffering the backlash of drugs and alcohol, we were glad to be here.

"This should be phenomenal," I thought.

I knew it'd be special, not to mention the fact that, we'd never played a gig at a resort like this.

I heard one guy said,

"It's the "Rock" event of the year!"

Rockin' Nam

SIDENOTE: I recently I had the distinct pleasure of talking to Steve Bell by phone—forty-three years later! I got a hold of the former correspondent's email and sent him a phone number. A few weeks later, I got a call. It was one of the great highlights of my life. We talked for quite a while. He told me that he remembered me, and the band. We talked about 'Nam, how I got there, how he got there. Also, how long he was there and how many tours he did. I sent him a copy of the book.

As for the footage, he didn't think it ever saw the light of day. In March, 2014, I sent Steve Bell a book, a blues' CD, a bio and resume, and a promo picture. He seemed to like it. We talked about a visit, a sit-down and catch up after forty-three years. As of now, we're trying to get together to have the "Reunion of a lifetime." I truly believe that a get-together like that would make this story complete.

I never dreamed all these years that something like this could happen. To meet up with the very newsman that filmed us? It will be great closure to this story, something very rewarding. I think the world of Steve Bell, not only because I met him over in Nam but because I followed his career back in the States on ABC programs.

Meanwhile, back at the ranch...Correspondent Bell was so impressed with us that he helped arrange a concert the next afternoon. Around 3 p.m. the following day, we all gathered in a funky auditorium to perform for a hundred Vietnamese teenagers—ALL GIRLS!

The band was to play for an hour—a private concert for these teens. They were very hip, dressed in jeans and Ts. They were screaming after every song. We were like teen idols! In fact, at times, I swear it felt like we were the Beatles! They were so happy and appreciative that we came out to play for them. It was unbelievable.

The next gig was a little farther north in Vietnam's oldest and its original capitol, Hue. Most of the guys slept on the way up. We did just an average show that night, but we *DID* get there, and we *DID* do the show. It wasn't horrible, just not as "electric" as some of the other gigs (how *could* it be?).

We did our best to use the energy we had left to try and rock these guys. My sentiment was: "just *do* what you can do." The following night was to be in the northern-most city in South Vietnam—the infamous, Dong Ha ... very remote. It was so "out-there", we wondered,

"What's *THIS* gig gonna be like?"

Turns out, it was *another* great gig. They welcomed the band like we were kings. It was awesome. Dong Ha was an interesting place. We did it in front of a great crowd outside, after chow, around 7 p.m. Dong Ha was the last town you come to before you get to the river and border of North Vietnam.

In fact, if you walk out to the edge of the complex, you could see the North Vietnamese flag flying on the other side of the Mekong River. It was so remote, that oftentimes, they couldn't get all the supplies up to camp. So on this particular night, the army prepared water buffalo for dinner.

Rockin' Nam

We finished eating and then it was time for the show. We started to play close to sundown, very cool. The guys were digging it. With about three songs to go in the show, after the GIs—seated on the dirt and grass for as far as you could see—were through applauding, from the distant trees you could hear some other faint applause. It was a little scary, but I never *really* worried. I mean, who's going to shoot the guitar player?

My entire time in-country, the sentiment was, "Who's going to snipe a musician?" but the next couple songs, I listened very intently and the sounds from the tree-line got louder. I don't think anyone caught onto this and I didn't want to seem like Shatner's character seeing the monster on the wing of the plane in *Twilight Zone*. I asked the band about this after the gig, and they thought I was out of my mind. They ribbed me about it for weeks. They never let me forget it.

We had a break for a couple days and then—a huge gig—the big reunion in Don Zume. It was going to be epic! We couldn't wait ... my home unit, the 577th Engineer Battalion. I was a little nervous but excited at the same time.

When we got into Don Zume, it was a love fest. The guys were ecstatic to see me. It was good to see them, as well. However, I felt a little depression. There was a sad vibe—in the atmosphere. I asked Gibo,

"What's going on?"

"They closed it down, all the privileges ... you know, to the Ville," he said.

I was bummed. Everyone was dragging ass, and I felt bad. This was my town ... these were my people.

"Not good," Stash said. "They've gotten strict."

They're making us play ARMY! ... No more wandering into the Ville ... no one gets high; no one gets laid."

"Wow" I shouted. "Well, let's try and have some fun tonight. It's so great to see you guys," I told them.

It was sad. They didn't deserve this. It seems the whole mood at the 577th was different than before, very different. It seemed cold and distant, so different than the first time I ever played there.

It was a warm night at the compound. A bunch of the guys were starting to gather. We got ready for the show. As I recall, I was probably a little more nervous on this gig than most, but looking out in the middle into the crowd and noticing that all the guys were groovin'.

We did our usual set. I remember that the show wasn't bad, but it probably wasn't as good as it could have been. Perhaps I was trying too hard or fatigue had caught up. Nevertheless, my friends seemed to like it.

Afterward, we all gathered on top of Sunshine's hooch. We talked and laughed for hours.

After getting high, catching up, and yakking it up, we got the munchies. We headed for the mess hall. It was somewhere around midnight. We broke in and raided the walk-in. There I was in civilian clothes—with a bunch of my friends, and making a ham sandwiches and other goodies. Just before we were done, guess who walks in? *Cap and his friends! Wow!* He didn't say a thing ... just gave us a weird look. I'm sure he really wasn't in the mood to see his old gas pumper in his kitchen eating and carrying on. He gave off some kind of strange vibe. All that water under the bridge with Cap, and he doesn't even say hello—bummer. He didn't even have to speak.

Rockin' Nam

He was like…

"Yeah, well, you weren't that good tonight, and now you're in my kitchen in bell-bottoms and faggoty outfits, stealing food, and acting like a bunch of hippies."

We were just trying to relax and get our "munchie" on. We slid out of there as quickly as possible. We moved the party back to Sunshine's hooch and I got to catch up with the rest of the guys; it was great! I never got tired of hangin' with them.

But it was so odd to be a soldier, then a star ... then back to being a soldier … overnight. Finally it got late, and as you can imagine, everyone was ready to crash. I found a bed and just laid there. I thought about the week, and what a week it was—so many memories to cling to.

The following day, we had more time off and I chose to spend it in Don Zume. It was so comfortable—the base I loved and was used to. I wanted to be with my buds, and as we partied through afternoon, something else substantial happened.

An old friend, Jake—very tall, big-hearted, good guy—came walking over very slowly after chow and mail call. He was very depressed and deliberate with his head down, and sat at the end of the roof. Not a lot of guys noticed.

"What's the haps, man?" I asked.

Jake could hardly speak. He just showed us the letter he'd received during mail call, after chow. Couple guys read it, and it wasn't good. Seems his wife of three years was tired of waiting around and met someone else. Word got around quickly, and Jake just sat at the end of the roof with his head in his hands.

He started bawling his eyes out. He was trying to hide it. He was drinking an orange NEHI. He was looking like he was capable of doing something rash. I was trying to think of a way I could help.

He was a good friend and a great guy. I tried to lighten up the situation by telling him a humorous story about a girl I knew just before the army took me away. I told him the story of how she sent me a minister certificate to try to exempt me from service.

I'm not sure what was rolling around in her head but it was strange. Anyway, she was layin' some shit on me.

"She was a little crazy—but cute. She loved the music, and we used to roll around like a couple of wild otters. I remember fun times those Saturday mornings. However, it turns out she had a problem with guys going into the military."

I continued,

"She went to the trouble of buying me one of those 'church minister' certificates by mail. It was from the Universal Life Church. She was trying to help get me out of the draft. It was one of those "mail-in documents." She had sent it to New Orleans. (I still have the ENVELOPE addressed to me at the apartment...in NEW ORLEANS)!

In protest to her issues about my particular situation, I took the liberty to send her a message. I proceeded to tell him how I filled the certificate out and proceeded to write, 'PAST-HER CHERRY' on the line.

"I sent it back to her. I thought it was funny. Nobody's sure if she ever got it. Hey! It's the thought that counts!

Rockin' Nam

Even if she didn't get it, I thought it was hilarious and worth it to make my point and get it back to her in a comedic way—to make a point. I wasn't trying to be mean, but I wanted to make a statement that it was *MY* life and I wasn't going to be swayed. Anyway, I hope I was successful."

"It gets better" I said.

"I sent her a letter from Seattle. I explained to her that not only did I go into the service, but I was on my way to Vietnam."

She wrote back one more time about how disgusted she was with me being involved in miliyary, Nam, and whatever else. I wish I could have seen her face as she was reading the letter. What a crack-up.

Needless to say, I didn't get any more letters from her."

"I NEVER HEARD FROM HER AGAIN!"

Everyone was digging my story. Jake was too. He seemed to mellow a bit. I was just trying to do my part to ease his pain. He didn't deserve this. He wasn't even supposed to be here. He had flat feet, and they told him they'd give him an "out." He joined us anyway. I always thought it was a shame that someone had to be ten thousand miles from home and deal with that kind of shit. How helpless is that? That evening, as usual, we gathered on the roof, (our usual ritual).

The roof that was made of old tin and sandbags, we noticed that Jake was still hurting. One by one, guys would offer a hopeful lament. It didn't seem to make much of a dent.

Rockin' Nam

We kept trying to lift Jake's spirits, but so far, no luck. This kind of thing seemed to be happening more and more as this conflict in 'Nam dragged on. But why did it have to happen to *THIS* guy? Why did it have to happen to Jake?

Although I didn't have a girlfriend or anyone waiting back home, it made me realize what those ten thousand miles in-between us meant. It was eerie, and it was ugly. You get the feeling that a certain someone you left at home waiting was trying to be patient, but for some, as they saw the blood and guts.

The people on the TV were mostly "Anti-war" so, no one ever got a proper perspective and it was just a matter of time until the wife would give up and find somebody else—someone closer to home—someone not connected with all "that."

Either way, it's not good news for any party all the way around. Everyone's breaking point was different, but as the lonely days went by, and the battle of boredom, solitude, and crazy thoughts festered, some of those waiting at home would cave. This was really one of the silent killers associated with this conflict. It was something that not many talked about.

However, if you were in the middle of it, you knew exactly how devastating it was—a real tragedy. There was a lot to be said about sitting helpless 10,000 miles away.

As for Jake, it was a cruel thing to put over on a dude who was trapped in this god-forsaken place and not even of his own doing. But we were bound and determined not to let him slide into the jaws of depression.

161

Rockin' Nam

As we sat on the roof, (our ritual), all of a sudden a song came on the radio. Most of us had portable stereos. It was a great diversion, and the price was right. Everyone had these things: drugs, stereos, girls.

The music was at low volume, on a huge silver AM/FM player. Everyone had a stereo. (They were pretty cheap. We bought a lot of them, Japanese made, and we got them cheap and fast. What else were we going to do with our $168 a month?)

Music was a huge part of military life in Vietnam. During this era in the war, AFVN did a great job playing some fantastic tunes; I'm not cutting them down. They blazed a great trail by playing some hits of the day, but also, a lot of "album cuts." It's just that a lot of us wanted our own stereos to play our own cassettes in the privacy of our own quarters.

As the song began to play, we knew it was Eric Burdon. It was a song we'd heard a lot. I don't blame the DJs at AFVN radio for playing this so much. In actually, it WAS a kind-of mantra in country. It was, in reality, a song that most GIs sang out loud every time it came on. I wanted this to be a great healing point for Jake!

I felt that if we could just create a very friendly moment, we could distract him for a period of time, maybe we could parlay it into a healing vibe. The longer we could get his mind off of this horrible situation, the more we had a chance to "save" him. We were trying our best!

I turned the stereo up louder. I felt like blaring out the music to strengthen the mood. We needed to "rock" our friend and take his mind off things. I turned it up just in time to hear the refrain as we sang along…

Rockin' Nam

"My little girl, you're so young and pretty ... and one thing I know is true ... you'll be dead before your ..."

More guys singing ...

"He's been wooooorkin', yeah, Wooooorkin', yeah ..."

Everyone was in now...

"Work, Work, Work, Work, Work ..."

At this point, we got to the chorus, and you could hear the big finale...

"WE GOTTA GET OUTTA THIS PLACE ... IF IT'S THE LAST THING WE EVER DO ... WE GOTTA GET OUTTA THIS PLACE ...

I managed to look over, and Jake is singing along! How great was that!

Then I finish it,

"GIRL THERE'S A BETTER LIFE ..."

Hey, we rocked him back to health!

There wasn't a dry eye on the roof!

Rockin' Nam

WOODSTOCK IN NAM
8.

The memories of Nam were always pretty vivid, but one incident really stood out. It was an ordinary week day and we were just getting into the "Saigon tour." We had landed somewhere up north and had just finished chow. We were a little tired but getting ready to play for the guys in a fairly secluded wooded area. It was dusk and things were a little unorganized but we were used to setting up in any circumstance and do our show. As we milled around something strange was about to happen.

I was chatting with some guys when, all of a sudden, sirens started going off. Everyone started scurrying. I wasn't used to this. I started to get concerned. I was taken aback, to say the least. All at once, we were ordered to get inside of this armored vehicle, you know the big tank with the huge gun sticking out of it. As I hovered inside with some others, I tried to stay composed, but I wondered what would have happen if we would have gotten pummeled with enemy gun fire. I mean, really… I thought,

"What if an enemy unit came in and wiped the whole camp and I'm there sitting in the tank?" We wound up sitting inside there for a good hour. I heard some activity outside but couldn't really make out what it actually was. When it came to that "Army" kind of stuff, I was pretty naïve.

Rockin' Nam

I just wasn't up on the "military-related" part of this duty. I mostly concentrated on entertaining my fellow soldiers and doing my best to make them all smile for a minute. As the band was finishing up the last of the Saigon gigs, we headed down south to the Delta region. We were approaching the late stages of the big tour and had only a few gigs left.

After a couple days off, I decided to stop into Saigon and visit Doug. I wanted to tell him all the highlights. On my way over, I thought I'd stop and buy some "Park Lanes." I'd always heard about them but never tried them. Park Lanes were store-bought, legal marijuana cigarettes that were sold from place to place. They came in regular cigarette-like packages and mostly sold in the city. I heard they were pretty good—kind of brittle— but pretty good. The guy at the store didn't have any packs left, but for a small price, he told me I could have a couple of singles from his private stash. I took him up on it and put them in the top pocket of my fatigue shirt.

I thought nothing of being AWOL (even though my tour was over and my papers were out of date). But hey, I was in the band. Who's going to mess with a music guy—or even *care* about me? I just wanted to have fun and do what I did. This carefree attitude would eventually catch up with me.

Making my way over to Doug's, the shit finally hit the fan. It got me. All of a sudden, a jeep full of MPs pulled up, and they demanded to see my ID and orders. Of course, the survivor in me took over. In a gruff voice, they told me that my orders were expired and asked me why I was wandering around.

In fact, they surrounded me and told me to take everything out of my pockets and place them on the hood of the jeep. I didn't panic, but I thought—"Thank God I don't have any powder on me, but WAIT—what about the Park Lanes?" Ever so slowly and methodically, I pull out every article I had in every pocket as slowly and deliberately as I could.

It was almost hilarious. I was desperately trying to kill time while fiddling with my pockets. In-between each move, I reached into my top pocket, like I was going to pull something out, but what I was basically doing, in reality, was slowly and purposely crushing up the brittle Park Lanes into crumbs while trying to distract the MPs all the while.

I was really procrastinating now ... gum ... comb ... pen ... (like the Paul Peterson tune). By the time I got to the last item, there was only tobacco shavings in my pocket and guess what? I just let the residue fall out of the pocket like they were old cigarettes. I pulled it off! *I DID it.*

I was really in a groove. I'd become so *good* in sticky situations! However, when I showed them my orders, the dates had expired, and I WAS in violation. I was officially AWOL, so they cuffed me and took me away. They drove me to a creepy facility. It was in a dark and remote part of Saigon. I'd never seen or even heard of it. It was an old jail used by the Vietnamese in the Indo wars. I was going to spend some time locked up. The facility had several cells; I was put in one of them. I can't even begin to describe how vile the place was. The walls were yellow from urine. There was nothing but a cement slab with a hole to pee.

Rockin' Nam

I constantly heard noises, moans, and other eerie sounds. I sat in this 5 x 5 space. The smell was so bad. So, once a rocker, in the company of friends and fans, I was now locked up. I was being punished for some reason (probably more than having out-of-date papers).

Of course, only later I would find out what the real reason for my incarceration was—that I was a goofball, an "a-hole", and constantly out of uniform. I sat in the corner of the cell trying to compose myself. I would later discover that while I was detained for expired papers, the reason for the arrest was the fact I was out of uniform and posed for photos while flipping everyone off—that and my general pompous attitude.

Apparently, those pictures I took go into the hands of the wrong people. They came back to haunt me...the pictures of me with the California flag and giving the finger were a definite thorn in my side. Somebody—somewhere—saw the photos and decided to put PFC Flyn on the "shit list," and here I am.

As the sun went down, and it got later, I started to lose my composure. I'd been taken to a part of the city (now operated by the military), booked, and embarrassed. I asked how long I might be there; the answer was—

"Until we get word to your unit," they said. Since there were no phones, I asked,

"How you going to do that?"

"We'll send a memo up with one of the convoys going north."

I started to sink deep. It occurred to me I might be there for a long time. I definitely needed some help— a break or something.

Rockin' Nam

Later that night, they announced that if there was anyone who wanted assistance with a drug or alcohol problems, that we were welcome to visit the medic and get help. I jumped all over this offer. My thinking was; that while I was out in public, even for a short time, I might find a loophole and maybe get a chance to change my fate. I'd gotten out of a lot of things; how was I going to get out of this one? We were taken over to a medical facility, and there I found a very attractive nurse on duty.

In private, I told her that I was kind of a big deal. I told her about the band, the tour, et cetera, and could she PLEEEEESE get me out of this, maybe use some pull. I gave her the best "sad-eyed" sob story I could think of. I don't think it did any good. I tried the dramatic approach. It was a no go! I was becoming desperate...What else could I do to get out of this? The situation always made me think of the scene out of *The Godfather*— the character played by Abe Vigota—

"Tom, can you get me off the hook, for old time sake?"

She sympathized with me but said there was nothing she could do. She was very soft and sweet about it, but the answer was still "no" (similar to Tom Hagen, a character played by Robert Duvall) —*"Can't do it, Sally ... can't do it."*

I couldn't believe it. I gave her my best lines, and my best resume and it got me nowhere. So now what? Now, I was really SCREWED! I remember waiting patiently that night and hoping that a lot of time would go by.

Rockin' Nam

I was hoping that the visit would drag on and on so I'd be exhausted when I got back. In the end, it was only about an hour, and what did they do for me? *THEY GAVE US DARVON! ARE YOU KIDDING ME?* Really? Darvon? Like that's gonna do any good! I didn't know much about medicine, but this was ridiculous.

It was almost like they were trying to bullshit us. Darvon? Seriously? Wasn't it merely a placebo! I guess they thought the soldiers would fall for this and think they we ok.

We all piled back into the vehicle and headed back to "Stalag 17." I was really getting concerned, and Darvon wasn't going to make a dent. I took two or three pills and thought,

"This may not be the scariest thing I've gone through, but it's one of them … How will I manage to go to sleep?"

Somehow, I drifted off for a few hours. Amazing I could sleep with all the stress, and all. I'm not sure how I kept it all together, but my patience was wearing thin, and I was bound to snap in due time. I woke up ugly. I sat up to an announcement that it was time for everyone to spend their "one-hour a day" out on the patio. I was pretty shaky by now but getting outside in the fresh air was probably going to do me a lot of good. I started trembling, and I felt like I might be losing it. I went out to get some air and I wasn't outside ten minutes—when suddenly—an older gentleman in civilian clothes was eyeing me.

"Who the fuck is *this* guy?" I thought.

Next thing I know, he wandered over and sat down next to me.

"You're the musician."

"What ... how did you know?" I asked.

"I'm unofficial," he mutters.

"WAIT! WHAT? Can you get me out of here? Why am I in here, anyway?" I asked.

"You got some attitude, don't you? He said. "Did you take an 'out-of-uni' pic ... flipping everyone off?"

"Maybe, I said ... but how petty?"

I don't know what the reason was…maybe the drugs, who knows? He proceeded to give me that talk, (like the park bench talk Donald Sutherland's character played in *JFK*… or maybe Hal Holbrook in *The Firm*. He continued asking if the drugs were good. I had no idea what he was getting at.

I told him that we heard someone back home was making a fortune shipping drugs, along with gold, silver, and assorted materials back to the US. I told him that it was hard to believe that the US would spend so many years and so many lives in a little country like Vietnam. He told me I shouldn't be concerned and to just concentrate on what I did best, "rocking the troops."

As far as the drug thing, he told me to forget it.

"Don't ask questions," he warned.

"Besides, there are reasons others have gotten whacked, and look, you don't really need to know about any of this.

It doesn't really concern you, and you're better off NOT KNOWING! There's an agenda over here, and you need to just keep your nose clean and concentrate on what you do best," he continued.

Rockin' Nam

I'm not quite sure what he was trying to say, but it appeared that he'd definitely seen his share of shit in "The Nam" and elsewhere. He was aged and weathered. He looked like a catcher's mitt with confidence. Only weeks later did I begin to put two and two together. But something was up with this guy.

"There's a reason the US has been here since the late fifties, but just mind your business, rock your music and ignore what you hear. Let others worry about it. You'll be way better off just being your goofy, 'innocent' self and doing great things for those guys," he said.

I just stared at him like a deer in the headlights. Like a kid from the warmth of the suburbs, I had no idea what he was saying. I was confused. I just wanted out. He left telling me to appreciate each day and realize the talent I had, what my role was, and what the music meant to the GIs.

"You and your music are very valuable to these guys and this cause. Don't waste it by running around flipping people off."

"Can you get me out of here?" I begged.

"I'll see if I can talk to somebody. Wise up. Get it right. Figure it out! You're here for a reason."

I didn't know where this guy came from. I didn't know why in the world he was here or how he got here. The guards were now signaling everyone to go back in. I looked around to say goodbye—and POOF—he was gone! Before I got up to go back, I sat there and decided to talk to God. It was my last resort. I promised Him that if He let me out of this, I would get my shit together. I vowed to straighten up, stop partying, and try to finish out my time in a better way…A much better way. As everyone started back to their cells, shockingly I was singled out. I heard the sergeant call out my name.

"FLYN!"

I approached the desk.

"FFC, you can go," he said

"WHAT?" I asked incredulously.

"Now go on; get out of here—GO! Before I change my mind!"

"Unf'n'-believable … I get to just WALK OUT? … No truck, no jeep, no nothing? Who was responsible for letting me out? Was it the guy? Was it God? Jeez!"

I walked outside, called a cab, and headed straight for Doug's. I couldn't wait to tell him all about what I went through! I got there and prattled on like a *teenager*—CRAZY

Again, Doug and I spent quality time together. I told him about the third tour and that I couldn't believe I was gonna be on my way down south for—yet—another tour. Now it was on to Can Tho and parts unknown.

What would *THIS* tour be like? It's so damn fun so far, I can't imagine … time to re-organize and get ready. We talked a lot about music, future plans, and how we were going to get together when we got "back to the world."

I was thrilled to be able to regroup for a minute and relax. When I got back, I discovered that Cap was gone. So were a lot of my buddies. It was like a ghost town. I tried to keep a low profile but I really didn't know how to act. And I wasn't very good at just sitting and bidding my time. I didn't even have to pack because I NEVER UNPACKED!

Rockin' Nam

A couple days later, we went south and finish the tour. Morning came quickly, and with new orders and the new Cap busy, I caught a ride on the mail jeep. It was a smart move. I jumped in, and we wound up leaving around 8:30 a.m. The mail man left the mail for the 577th, and we pulled out. My plan was to fly from Dalat to Saigon on Air Viet Nam (with my own money).

I was going to try to stop at Doug's. It was time to reconnect with him anyway. On a beautiful day, the mail guy and I got along nicely. We chatted up a storm as the new day was just breaking. I bonded like this with many soldiers. All of a sudden, my CO (Captain "way pissed off") — was on the horn.

"Yes, Captain," the Jeep driver answers.

"Is Flynn with you?" comes over the radio.

"Oh SHIT!" I said. "He got the mail!" I could hear him over the CB.

I started motioning wildly.

"NO" I said to the driver (my new best friend).

"Ah, no, sorry Cap, I've already dropped him.

"Shit!" is what I heard on the other end.

"Are you sure?" asks the angry CO.

"Yeah, I dropped him a little bit ago."

"Do you know where you dropped him?"

"Well, I have to catch him, where is he?"

"NOT DALAT! I moaned.

"Well, um … one of the units along the way, Sir," said the mail guy. "I can't remember."

ANYWHERE BUT DALAT!" I whisper.

"Alright, thanks,"   the CO answered.

I was so relieved. I thanked the Jeep driver many times over. The driver said he was glad to do it.

Rockin' Nam

I got dropped off at the tiny airport in Dalat, and got out. I offered the guy some money. He refused and said he was happy to help out a "bro."

I had some extra money on me. That was cool. These extra funds allowed me to buy a ticket as a civilian and fly normal. I purchased a one-way on an Air Viet Nam flight to Saigon. It wasn't very expensive, and it was a nice break. Before the flight, I spent an hour up in the restaurant of the control tower. Everyone had gathered for lunch, so I wound up ordering noodle soup. I mingled with all the locals who were traveling.

This was such a strange little place. So beautiful yet so complicated … so innocent, yet so exploited. As we all boarded the plane, the craft was small. I could hardly fit inside (and I was skinny). The flight cracked me up. A gorgeous stewardess served up tiny Dixie cups of punch and a couple of mints, but the flight wound up being smooth. I thought about flirting with her but decided to keep my mind on the tour.

After an interesting flight, I landed at the airport in Ben Hoi. I got a ride over to Doug's and was feeling better than ever. However, upon arriving at Doug's place, something seemed weird. For the first time, he didn't seem like "Doug." It was weird. He didn't have very good news for me either. He told me that a lot of people were beginning to sour on me. I was pretty bummed and didn't want to hear it.

They were getting wind that the "big celebrity" (me) was a problem soldier, and a lot of people didn't want me around. Some were warned not to keep me on because I was in trouble. There seemed to be more and more rumors about me.

Rockin' Nam

They had heard about the "flipping-off" pictures and had expressed concerns. The rumor was that they heard I'd spent time in jail, and he didn't think they wanted me back. Seems they didn't want to get involved with a "problem"! I was quite aware of the "rep" I'd acquired. Doug suggested that I might want to scrap the trip. Whoa! What was he saying?

"You've always been a supporter of mine, and now you're suggesting I just turn around and go back ?"

"I can't do that...go back to the unit where the CO is waiting for me? That CO up there is out for blood!" I screamed.

"Look, I'm just saying that the word from the top is that they've soured on you," Doug answered.

I was floored, stunned, saddened. Well, there was no way in HELL I was NOT going to finish my concert tour. I politely said goodbye to Doug and made my way down south. Now I'm really freaking out. A million thoughts went through my head. After playing such great music and having so much success, why was this happening to me? All because of those stupid pictures? As it turns out, it wasn't JUST the pics. It was the reputation I'd acquired. Months of being a rebel, a wild man, an out-of-uniform, smart-mouthed soldier in the US Army finally caught up to me. However, when I *DID* arrive, it was amazing! The shocker of the century! The C.O. in the Delta was actually happy to see me! They welcomed me in with open arms! Inside, I thought,

"WHAT, the hell is going on here?"

This guy couldn't have been happier to see me. Were those rumors true? What the fuck! I couldn't believe it?

The promoter gave me a thumbs-up and said, "Let's finish the tour!"

"YES!" I said as I was elated!

We did a great first night back, and the people were impressed. Everyone was so celebrating the next day. Someone set up a trip to go downtown and buy some new band outfits.

"WHAT?" I thought … "new outfits?"

This turned out to be such a lucky break for me——timely too. To gain the freedom to score (drugs)!

It was quite beneficial because GIs were no longer able to wander into the Ville at anytime, besides, I knew I'd be leaving the country soon

The next morning, they carted the band down to some funky garment shop, run by a very funny and polite East Indian dude in an old rickety house. My ingenuity and desperation were already up and running. I was like an animal whose instincts just kicked in. I went into action. I really needed to get downtown if only for a little bit.

Over the months, I'd turned into quite the master manipulator. Incredibly, while the first guy was trying on some crazy two-toned, bell-bottomed jumpsuit, I went to the back door and snuck outside. I found some boy-san and told him I wanted some pot. The boy gestured for me to follow him. I darted down a dirt alley, and the kid brought me into an old shack. I pulled out money. I paid him and scooted with the goods. I did all this in a very rapid and concise manner. I quickly raced back to the building. I slyly snuck back into the rear door of the clothing place and thought,

"Man, what a feat!"

I gave the kid a nice tip, thanked him 'buku'. I headed back. How lucky. I just poke my head out the back and there's a kid ready to take my order. Sometimes, I'm even surprised. I very quietly and nonchalantly snuck back in like nothing had happened. I had turned into quite the genius. I think it was more like a survival kind of thing. I slowly moseyed over to the fitting area (like I just came out of the bathroom) just in time to hear,

"Flyn! ...Your turn!"

Hey! I just pulled off, THE IMPOSSIBLE!

I don't think anyone in the world realized that. This had to be one of the greatest schemes of all time!

Afterwards, the band acquired these ridiculous, two-toned, black and white, bell- bottomed jumpsuits. We headed out and made our way back to our quarters. I was happy and satisfied with a new tour—and a fresh supply of powder and shitty outfits. What more could a guy want?

I had lot of talent in many areas, but fashion was *not* one of them. These outfits were HIDEOUS! They were mostly my idea, and it's a damn good thing that pictures of those outfits didn't follow us around. What a crack up. How embarrassing it would have been if anyone ever saw this and snapped a few pictures off.

In retrospect, everyone in the band was glad that no one outside of the Delta region in 1971 saw these clown suits. I was feeling good.

I strolled through the complex before the show. I swear I looked like shit, dirty dingy, and, in fact, funky as hell. I had on half a uniform, beads and jewelry, and more cockiness that ever as I walked along.

Rockin' Nam

As I was strutting across the base, I was surprised to run into an old friend … well, acquaintance, actually. It was someone I hadn't seen in a long time. It was — Needlewick! And, he didn't recognize me! He just looked at me and said,

"Son, are you in the army?"

"Yes sir, unfortunately I am," I answered.

He went on like a fool. As if I was going to listen to what he had to say.

"Well, I want you to get cleaned up…get your hair cut, and report to my office at exactly 0200 hours …"

I cut him off midsentence —

"Yeah, I'll be sure to do that, MacArthur.

He screams, "What? Wait! Where do you think you're going? I'm going to turn you in for insubordination!" I could still hear him yelling shit as I chuckled and walked on down the way.

This was hilarious … to run into that "jag-off" way down here, AND HE DOESN'T EVEN RECOGNIZE ME! I turned forty-five degrees and vanished immediately from view.

The ensuing shows went fairly smoothly all week, nothing earth-shattering but steady nonetheless. This tour was not as dynamic as the previous ones. Still, we *were* happy to be there … and to play music. We were glad to just be back on the road.

As we got down to the last of the gigs, one thing was alarming. It seemed apparent I was losing quite a bit of my MUSIC MOJO. I still loved to rock, but I was getting more complacent lackadaisical, maybe bored about everything, including my gigs. This was very apparent on a night in late summer of 1971.

Rockin' Nam

I really fucked up. On one of our final shows when I screwed up big time. I started taking things for granted. I had definitely veered off. I'm thinking of all I'd been through, and that I knew I was getting "short" and deep down I was mad I hadn't stopped partying.

On this particular evening, I had a girl in my quarters. That was my first mistake. It was about an hour before show time. I was trying to have sex but was taking my time. All of a sudden, I was running out of time. I was really pushing the envelope now. It was late, and I just wanted to "get off" before the show. I had to get her out and get my ass to the stage.

At this point, I was still in a good frame of mind, but I was in trouble. Arrogance and stupidity got the better of me. I finally got my shit together but, sadly, it was too late. I raced over to the facility. I heard music coming from the inside which could only mean one thing — the band had started! — and without me! What in the world was I thinking?

I crept into the building and saw the crowd watching the band play ... WITH ONLY THREE MEMBERS! I slithered onto stage, trying to blend in with the band without anyone seeing me...fat chance, no way. I tried to fade into the song, to blend in, but couldn't. I peeked up at the band, and they just stared at me and looked down shaking their heads...bummer, and they were doing a LONG set. It was very sad to be in this predicament with my band, but I only had myself to blame.

I think it's safe to say I had now gone **WELL** beyond those two "freaks" I met earlier in my "Nam" experience in Cam Ranh.

After the show, the civilian promoter, (who was there at the gig), came up to me and fired me. He expressed disappointment, told me that the band was great, but he couldn't have me running rough-shod through these gigs. I told him I understood and thanked him for the chance. I walked away devastated. It was like a bad dream! I wondered what my fate would be. Where would I go? What would I do?

How far would it go? Was it REALLY time to go home? How would I get by? I wandered away as sad as someone could be. It was my own fault and I was about to take a good long look at myself. I returned to Saigon and to Doug's.

However, when I arrived, I found out that Doug's time was up. He had gone. I was devastated. It seemed his obligation was over and all those memories were just that ... memories. It meant he was heading "back to the world."

I was in a deep depression now. I never got to say goodbye. I was crushed. I sat in private and cried my eyes out. The great, great times we had together, the guy that brought me down there—my rock in the middle of the big city—were all gone! And it ended badly—on such a sour note!

I roamed around a little, but my heart wasn't in it. It was getting late, and I did not want to travel. Besides, the convoys never made trips that late anyway. I decided to borrow a Jeep and drive out to the airport.

Rockin' Nam

Out at the Bien Hoa airstrip, I approached the brightly colored lights, and it made me feel better. I turned the Jeep off and just sat there. I could see the planes land. Down the runway and then take off again…made me so sad! I could also see the jets come in and land. Every time I watched a jet take off, it gave me chills. At times, my eyes teared up, and I'd get lonely and melancholy. I had always been a sucker for an airplane. This goes back to my childhood.

As I sat there at the airport for a few hours, I started to reflect and try to make sense of the crazy year. It truly was *one* wild time. I thought about going to the medics for some help to get rid of this depression.

I thought about that guy on the jail patio was trying to say. I tried to feel proud of what I had accomplished. After all, I *DID* make a lot of soldiers happy. The band DID take them back to the world for an hour or so.

For a brief time, we rocked their world. I became very introspective and for the first time. I think I was finally starting to figure out *why* I came to 'Nam — …What my mission was in this US Army and in Nam. No, it wasn't the partying, but I *did* start to put it all together. It all made sense now. I figured out that I had God-given talent and I was to share it with fellow soldiers. It was sinking in. I had such an array of emotions, so much happiness from the good times, many memories — high and low.

Rockin' Nam

I started getting emotional again. Every time I'd try to straighten out, I'd become a wreck. As I felt so low, I watched a 707 fly overhead and cry my eyes out. Earlier, I saw couples walking down the street holding hands, and I'd get all weird and homesick. Just then, a guy came on the radio...

"Sad news today Rockers ... Jim Morrison was just found dead in his hotel bathtub in Paris, France."

I turned the radio off. How bad could it get? Later that night, before I was to return to Dom Zume, I met some new buds. They were hanging out in some barracks in the Saigon vicinity. They started partying, and I fell right in. It felt good a bunch of guys who had gathered to party, and they were having a good time.

One of the guys had seen the band some time ago. I was starting to feel normal again. All of a sudden, a guy walked in. Apparently he was a friend and came in, looked like hell, and hung his head —

"What's up, bro?" someone asked.

"My best friend is DEAD!" he sobbed.

"NO WAY!" I yelled.

With tears in his eyes, he proceeded to tell us this incredibly, hard-hitting story.

"He met an ugly and vile end — AND — just few days before he was to go home. According to his friend, he was really hooked on the stuff because it was even

183

harder to get into the Ville. Everyone was hurting, but he was hurt the most. According to his friend at the '1st Cav,' he had snuck off to go looking for white powder. He couldn't get over that things weren't like the old days. He had so much trouble adapting to the 'New' Nam. He was having trouble finding any "stuff."

He traipsed around the village for more than hour," he mumbled. "He was caught and brought back and punished him by making him do shitty detail for three days. He was going out of his mind."

"About a week later, he went out again.

He had met a connection. He snuck out. He was like a rabid dog. It is said that he wandered around a while but then went deeper into some village and found a mama-san who told him she might have a couple vials for fifty bucks." (He would have paid anything).

"She told him to come by, and they'd make the deal. In the morning, he was nowhere to be found. Alarms started going off and questions were asked. When he came up missing, everyone was concerned. Now they ALL went looking for him. At first they were on a wild-goose chase."

He went on…

"They got frustrated because they didn't know whether someone was covering for him. Maybe they JUST didn't care because it was 'drug-related'. The team started sensing that there was something fishy going on, but they just couldn't figure it out."

"With the lack of communication and the fact they were basically in the 'back woods,' they came up empty time and again, no evidence to be found! They looked everywhere but not two nights later, they finally found him in a very remote area. They found him on his back. He was down by the creek with a shitload of white foam oozing out of his mouth. Apparently, he scored a couple vials, and it became fatal for him. It is told that our friend took a huge snort."

This guy was a wreck now. He could hardly speak but went on to explain the details…

"He died almost immediately. I guess the drug dealer was VC and had filled it with *DRAIN CLEANER* that was white and looked similar to the real stuff. He snorted it up, and as it was sucked up through his nasal cavity and into his brain, it hit him."

"He was instantly poisoned."

(Now the guy is shaking with tears in his eyes). He was about as shaken as anyone.

Apparently, everyone at the base was shocked, but they weren't sure WHY he died. The word around was that he just OD'd. There was no mention of VC posing as normal mama-sans selling to GIs and we hadn't really heard anything. I thought that up to now, it was relatively safe to cruise around. Jesus! I was shocked that such tactics were being used in this mess. I never dreamed it would get so sick.

Rockin' Nam

I started thinking,

"As if the GIs didn't have enough to contend with while they were over here doing who-knows-what in this Godforsaken land. This was pretty fucking scary and I'd be lying if I said I wasn't concerned.

That could have been me out there!

I went through some crazy shit, obviously. When the truth came out at the base, there was retribution. They sent an ugly message back to the other side. Not sure exactly what it was but it was pretty.

Was this real? Could it have been true? I did my best to try to forget it as quickly as possible. Sadly, some never took this to heart, and eventually they'd all stumble all the way to the end...

And believe me ... wind up paying for it!

One Night in Bangkok
9.

Somehow I made it back up to the 577th. When I got there, my old Cap was gone. Almost everyone I knew was gone. There were only a few guys left. What would I do now? I decided to use my trump card. I still had my one R & R in my back pocket (the Taipei excursion was just a "business trip"). Maybe now, I'd be able to go away, relax, dry out and get clean so I could pass that damn URINE test when it came time to go home. I knew my time was coming.

I went to my only two connections left in admin. They were so cool, always nice to me. They asked me,

"Where do you want to go, man?"

"Anywhere, just so I can leave soon," I explained.

"Well, let's see … I can get you to Bangkok tomorrow on a 2 p.m. out of Da Nang."

"Far out! I'll take it," I said.

He gave me a list of what I needed to do to get out of country to Thailand. There were a lot of "thank-yous" all around as they asked how the tour went. "Crazy," I lamented.

The sheet he gave me was a little eye-opening. Apparently, a GI has to fulfill five steps to get out of country, weather you're going home or just on R & R. It was nothing like this just a few months before. The five steps for leaving the country were as follows:

1. Have an up-to-date shot record …
2. Have civilian clothes …
3. Have at least $100 …
4. Have a military ID … and …
5. Pass a urine test before getting on the plane …

Well, I *HAD* an ID. I had civilian clothes—
plenty—in fact. I had some money but NO up-to-date
shot record. And, of course, it was obvious I wouldn't be
able to pass a piss test if I was drinking and smoking pot.
That night I made a trip down to the medics to see about
a shot record. When I got there, no one recognized me.
They were doing something secretive. When I took a
closer look, it looked like they were stuffing pine boxes
with something. I tried not to be shocked.

Someone walked over and asked me to wait in
another area. I obliged. After all, they were doing *me* a
favor. (A few years later, I would put two and two
together as they filled the caskets up with 'stuff' and
shipped it back to the States). The guy came over and
gave me a head nod.

"Help you, bro?"

"Sure," I said … "going on R & R tomorrow …
need a shot record."

"Oh, is that all?" the dude chuckled. "Wait here,
give me your ID."

A few minutes later, he came over with a brand
new, bright yellow, shot record.

"Here you go, man."

"Thank-you very much," I said.

I offered some money, but he said, "That's okay.

188

"Man, just helping out a bro ... have fun."

And just like that, I had a good, up-to-date shot record and went on to have a great night. I got high, got what I needed, and next morning got up and got rolling. The truck was leaving for Da Nang, and I was getting on it. I was now scheming on getting some more bucks, and I would deal with the urine test when I got there.

I started reflecting and reminiscing again on the way to Da Nang. I was thinking back to just a month ago when the band was here. I was thinking of how we were celebrities and getting filmed by ABC News. I thought about the guys back at base and all the strange days. Those were great days—and it was just a short time ago! No one in the truck recognized me, and I seemed to be pretty relaxed about that. I was in another mode now. I wanted to take care of biz and get my ass to Thailand.

When we got dropped off, there was an OD green colored bus taking GIs to the airport. It was packed with soldiers, some going on R & R, some going home. I was going on a very well-needed "vacay" to Bangkok. I was hoping to get "right" and have a break, see some girls, and experience another city.

When I got on the bus, it was a festive atmosphere. Everyone was in a great mood because they were leaving ... if only for a week! I found out who had money. Most of the guys were short on civilian clothes and, of course, I had a shitload. I quickly sold enough clothing to make over a hundred dollars. I wound up with more than enough cash. I then sat quietly on the bus ride and prayed to the Man upstairs.

That's right, another, prayer—

"God, if you let me get outta here, I promise I'll act right, and get ready to go home clean—I swear."

I finally got to the airport check-in-area. We all disembarked, and he followed the line to the gate. I felt a little tired and a little nervous. At this point, I was pretty much SPENT. I just need a little more luck and to somehow get by this and move on. As I approached the gate, the miracle I'd prayed for was in sight. The prayers were about to be answered. As I approached the gates, it was very hard to believe, but there was a huge sign that read:

"URINE TEST OUT OF ORDER TODAY"

Get out! Are you F'n' kidding me? This is unbelievable! We all marched to the lineup where a Pam Am 707 was to take off for Bangkok. There were other lines for different planes (some to Sydney, some to Taipei, some to Hawaii), but this was the plane for my trip. As I boarded, I was somewhat giddy. It was so hard to imagine that I prayed for this and it came true. I was truly on a roll. How long could my luck hold out? I couldn't believe I pulled it off! I found my seat, sat down quietly, and thanked the Lord for answering the request. It was unquestionably the biggest favor ever. I still can't get over it. Of course, I would ultimately go back on my promises, but at this point, I had the best intentions.

For now, I was in good shape. I was looking forward to a nice relaxing time in Thailand where I could take care of biz. I'd get some sleep … get straight … meet girls … rest up. Now it was time to chill, go out, sightsee, take it easy.

The landing gear was down as we made our final descent into Bangkok. It was nightfall. I saw a beautiful amber sunset from my seat on the plane. When we landed, I found my way to the shuttles and was taken to the Bangkok Hilton. It was a little straight and touristy, but I was ready to get settled. I checked in around 8 p.m. and was given a room on the 5th floor. I got in and started to feel a little "off." I thought—

"Maybe I'll take a bath, lie down for a while, and get a rest. A few minutes later, there was a knock on door. I opened it. A beautiful girl stood in the doorway.

"Do you want some company?"

"You're very pretty … but I'm just in and … no, not right now, OK?" I answered.

"Are you sure?" she insists.

"Yes, I'm sure … maybe I'll talk to you later."

"OK," she reluctantly said.

She had a pouty look on her face.

I closed the door and realized that might have been the first time I ever turned down the "choo choo."

I ran another bath and before you knew it, another knock on the door and, yeah, you guessed it— another girl. I also turned her down.

191

Rockin' Nam

I then called the desk and asked them not to send any more. They obliged. Again, I tried the bath and another knock on the door. This time, a young boy stood there wondering if I'd like some pot. He held out a little mound of emerald green pot. I scowled and rolled my eyes.

"Man I just came from 'Nam ... I get that shit by the burlap-bagsful for FREE!"

"But it is 'emerald green'," he claimed.

"OK, how much?" I ask.

"$40," he says.

"Get out!" I started to close the door.

"OK, OK," the kid says, "I'll make you a deal. I'll *give* it to you; you don't like, I don't charge you."

"I don't know." I stammer.

"Ah, c'mon ... take a chance," the kid says.

"Let me try it, and we'll go from there. You just leave the sample; I'll do a little, and I'll get back to you.

SIDENOTE: It's important to mention, at this point, that in these days, there's a hookah pipe in every room on the front table of most hotel rooms in Thailand. It was all very legal in the country. Hey, it was legal in "Nam" too. Well, that was a given. At least, in our area of where I was hanging out. In fact, they were just giving it away in some situations. I know that the ganja varied from place to place but seriously, how different could this be...really?

I agreed to take the pot on a trial basis. I put a pinch into the huge brass pipe and took a few tokes. It smelled wonderful. To be honest, there wasn't much to get excited about, and so I finally ran the bath. I climbed in, and laid back. I was spent...all the craziness of the far East. As I lay in the bathtub, it started to come on — and what a high.

"Damn, the kid was right."

It was a great bath and a nice high. I got out after a half hour and plopped down on the bed. I tried to find something on TV. There was nothing but crap on. There might have been some "pay movies," but they were expensive and with subtitles. There was just nothing on, and I thought I might get a good sleep. But in an hour, I would start feeling bad again. It seems that this partying withdrawal thing was rearing its ugly head again. I might have dropped off for an hour or so, but when I awoke, I was in real pain.

All I had was that pot, and the way I felt, I wasn't really interested in getting stoned again. I tossed and turned and writhed in discomfort ... twelve o'clock ... 1 a.m. ... 2 a.m. — I couldn't stand it. I decided I needed something stronger.

I poked my head out the door into the hallway. A boy-san was hanging around. I gave a motion. I told him that he'd better go get me some pills. He took my $40 and disappeared. It was more than an hour but it seemed more like days. The boy-san finally returned about 3 a.m.

Rockin' Nam

The kid disappeared again and didn't return until 4:30 a.m. He brought a small amount of whatever. He demanded another $20. I paid it and took it. It wasn't very good, but it got me through the night. I awoke feeling like shit. It was a night from hell. WHAT in the world was I to do? I had no idea what I was in for, but what happens next is truly SHOCKING!

After a few pathetic hours of sleep, I woke up about 11 a.m. I wasn't sure where I was or what I was doing but…I decided to go out … Out in the city and started enjoying myself. The city was beautiful in the midday sun. I met a whole bunch of people, mostly European. A guy on his bicycle was very friendly, and we bonded right away. After the usual chitchat, I asked him where he was staying. He gave me a business card from the hotel he was at (Euro-owned). He said it was about $1.75 per night (with a balcony). This was hard to believe since everything I've experienced so far was geared towards the vacationing military soldier … and expensive.

"This sounds right down my alley." I told him that I'd check it out for sure. I also explained that I had some gear back at the Hilton and would he mind coming with while I gathered my bags. I wanted him to go with me and get my belongings. He agreed, and off we went to my hotel to gather my shit then we could cruise back to his cool hotel he showed me. We headed for the Hilton. When we got there, the guy waited in the lobby while I ran upstairs to grab my shit. I wasn't gone but a minute or two, and when I came down, my new friend was GONE! ...Gone from lobby, gone from the hotel, gone like the wind—gone but not forgotten. I was a stunned. I looked around. Like a rooster, my head was craning in every direction. Just as I was about to take a look outside, the hotel manager summoned me. He motioned for me to come over to the desk. I slowly made my way. I noticed several Thai police gathering near the doorway. I started to freak. A dreadful chill ran up my back. I had a feeling something weird was about to happen. The answer suddenly popped into my head—

"Of course! THE INCIDENT IN THE MIDDLE OF THE NIGHT!"

Before I reached the front desk, I decided to make a break for it ... a mad dash to the side door. I quickly slipped out and ran down the street and jumped into a cab.

"Where you go?" the cabbie asks.

"Just go!" I yelled.

He sped off!

At the next light, Thai police cars pulled up.

"Really? No F'n' way!" I'm thinking.

This had become a dire situation!

As they talked (in Thai) to each other, I decided to jump out the one cab and run down another alleyway as fast as I could. I was really freakin' now. I made the decision to jump into yet another cab.

Rockin' Nam

I was really freaking out at this point. A million scary thoughts were going through my brain. What was to happen to me if they catch me? What kind of legal trouble would there be? I tried scooting down another alley. I felt they were close—on my ass. They were bound and determined to get me.

I jumped into yet another taxi. Again, I yelled for him to head down the street! We went a block or two, and here come the police again—and MORE of them! They also started conversing with each other in their native tongue. Guns were drawn.

I jumped out and began just jogging and blending in with the crowd. I ran down so many streets, I was delirious. It went on and on. At this point, I was running on nothing but adrenaline and fear. I was petrified. Did I realize the direness of this? Did I realize how much trouble I was in? I guess I didn't have much time to think about anything logical was just flyin' by the seat of my pants.

Some time ago I got information that scoring certain drugs in Thailand was a grave offense. I freaked some more. I decided to run down more streets and jump into more cabs. What an adventure I was mired in. A million thoughts crossed my mind in all this ...

"This was right out of the film, *The French Connection*, or other action adventures, I swear to God."

As I ran down yet another alleyway, I made a right, then a left, then another right.

196

Rockin' Nam

Finally I decided to really put it into high gear. I ran up and down, back and forth, and then, with no one in sight, jumped into one more cab and shouted — "AIRPORT!"

I ducked down in the back seat. I told him NOT to stop. The cabby drove a long time. The airport was a good 20-30 minutes out of town, way out on the edge. I *WASN'T* in a hurry to sit up. In fact, I was just as happy to lay in the back for hours, or even days, if that's what it took. Finally, I was pretty sure the coast was clear. I slowly sat up in the taxi. To my relief, low and behold, no one was behind us! They weren't following me! At least I was fairly sure.

By now, I was almost hysterical. Literally running for my life! SHIT! My pants were soiled from the huge urine spot right in the front of my Hagar slacks. As we approached the airport, I showed the cabbie the business card from the other hotel and said, "OK, STOP! ... Take me here."

I handed the cabbie the card to the Euro hotel. Bewildered and frustrated, the guy says,

"That far away ... other side of city,"

"It's OK, it's OK ... I pay, I pay," I told him.

I DID pay — with a good-sized tip. The taxi driver took me right to the hotel I wanted! In fact, the drive was actually pleasant. Except for the fact that I almost had a heart attack, got the firing squad, and peed my pants, I was OK.

I checked in and paid the small price for the room. The guy was right! It was small but nice—WITH A BALCONY! Relaxed now, excited and relieved, I opted to cruise around. I went down to the lobby and beyond. This place was incredibly better than where I was. The thought of getting away with losing those Thai officials BLEW MY MIND!

As I wandered around the rustic European-owned hotel, I see the Euro guy—the guy who gave me the card, the guy who bailed on me. I walked toward him and threw up my arms, as if to say, "WTF?"

"What happened? You bailed on me," I asked.

"So sorry, mate. They told me to go," he said.

"They said there might be trouble. I thought I should take off." He explained.

"Wow, I was running for my life out there and I barely escaped."I said shockingly.

"Well, you're here now, so welcome," he jokes.

I nodded with a semi-smile and went on my way. I was definitely in a better space now. I was under the radar and apparently safe. I went outside and bought a fresh pineapple juice Popsicle. It was very tasty, right from the real fruit.

That night, I went out to a cool disco complete with black lights and pretty girls. On this particular night, I DID meet someone—she was nice, cute, hip and nicely dressed with a great smile. For a minute there, I'd forgotten I was even in another country.

This was a familiar situation I was used to back home. We looked at each other. There was an immediate attraction.

"I'm Susie," she said.

"Hi Susie, I'm Flyn … do you want to sit down and chat for a little bit."

"Ok," she said with a smile.

I liked her. We had some drinks. Then I said—

"Shall we dance?

I can't remember if she spent the night, but we had a very fun night and I made sure she got home okay.

The next day I slept in and got up late. I was now getting some rest. One thing that freaked me out was that, while pot was 100 percent legal in Thailand. However, possession of any other drug brought the dire consequences. I thought about the ordeal at the Hilton. All week long, I hit the discos every night. It was becoming the week I had hoped for—and needed.

Toward the end of the week, I was getting very comfortable. It was finally beginning to feel like a wonderful R & R. On the final night, I met a really nice girl. Her name was Jill. She was Asian and spoke perfect English. She told me she was from New York and that her dad had gotten a civilian job in the Far East working with the government. We spent the last night at her place. She had a cool pad—a guitar, pillows, some wine, and I blew her mind when I picked up her guitar (a Yamaha or a Takamine). I started jamming.

She looked like she was impressed. We drank, played music, had some romance, and even got high. We talked about everything under the sun—from politics to music to films to pop culture—hours and hours! We covered just about EVERYTHING! I don't think we left anything out. In fact, we were SO into it that I completely lost track of time. Around seven in the morning, as we lay naked in her flat, I freaked.

"SHIT! I have to go ... gonna miss my flight!"

I gave her a hug and kiss, told her how great it was, that it was the best time, and maybe we could get together "back in the world."

The cab arrived, and it was time to go. I looked like shit. I was on a six-day party bender. And I really LOOKED like it. I got in the cab.

"Airport please!" I demanded.

I kept looking at my watch as this guy drove around and around, and I finally thought,

"WHAT THE FUCK? THIS GUY CAN'T FIND THE AIRPORT!"

I was having a fit—screaming and yelling. When I finally got there, it was insane. I got out, and THE PLANE WAS ON THE TARMAC! SHIT! I jumped out of the cab, ran towards the tarmac, until I saw the plane slow down. And in a shocking turn of events, THEY STOPPED FOR ME, AND I GET ON! Unbelievable!

I managed to make my flight! Can you imagine the faces of the guys on the plane? They looked like they just saw some kind of psycho get on board. I reeled and weaved to the back and sat down. I looked around and smiled, and then discovered I'd left my wallet in the cab!

"SHIT! MY WALLET!" I yelled.

"BUMMER, man," someone said.

"Fuck it. I'll sleep all the way back to Cam Ranh," I growled. Then I thought—

What was THAT?" Shit! What a week that was!

It was supposed to be a nice mellow week in Bangkok, and low and behold, it turned into this scary episode of *Kojak*. I lay back and tried to close my eyes but just couldn't get over what a crazy escapade I just went through in Thailand. What a week! I'm not sure if there was a wilder time for a GI on R & R.

When I got back, my new C.O had a message for me... Uh oh, was this another Needlewick and the fiasco in Cam Rahn?

"Flyn ... been looking for you. General Abrahams has requested you and your band to do a special show."

Really?" I gasped.

"HELL YES! Guys are fucked up all over Nam sick...suicidal...at the end...and they're putting a huge concert together! It seems they need you. There's a chopper here this afternoon to take you to Cam Ranh, then Saigon. Look, I don't know who you are, but you must be something special ... been calling every day."

He went on to say that he had many phone calls trying to find me, some from fellow soldiers—even some from a band member or two. He had a scowl on his face and I recognized the vibe. He already didn't like me because of attention I was getting. I knew how bad I looked when Cap said, "And clean yourself up ... you look like SHIT! General Abrahams arranged for our own C-130 to carry us.

I ran across the tarmac and heard the sound of the huge propellers booming. I lumbered up to the cargo door and threw my shit in. I managed to climb on board, and guess who was there to greet me? The band! We started celebrating and high fiving. We were giddy as hell. There we were, together again, the four of us. We spent the next hour rehashing, recalling, and catching up. We couldn't stop yakking. Some of them were going home also.

"Wow! Now, we always have our own C-130!"
...Just the pilot, the band, and a bombardier."
The bombardier couldn't have been nicer to us. He seemed proud to be part of helping us out and getting from here to there. It was an awesome reunion, I was happy. I was coming off some stressful times and it was good to get "right" again.

Arriving at Cam Ranh, before I caught a van over to my facility, General Abrahams (Westmoreland's guy in Nam) was there to greet the band and do a photo-op holding some certificate as he presented us with an award for what we had done for the troops. We met with the four-star general and he thanked us all for coming and doing this. We all said goodbye as I went to pack my stuff for the final time.

Rockin' Nam

ALL MY SORROWS
10.

Music played in the background. I recognized the song. It was the Doors' hit "Riders on the storm." It was from the new album, "L.A. Woman."

The band was nervously excited to get out on stage, to get in position, and get into a groove. We got out there and I got to the microphone. I looked out at everyone and I shouted:

"Hey, we're Rockin' it! We're Rockin' Nam!"

The crowd cheered wildly. We got tuned up, and it seemed that the crowd already thought we were something special. Were we? We loved being there, because THEY were something special! We had played for these guys all year long and we never got tired of it. They were the best.

You just can't imagine what kind of character one has until you see them up close and personal. We had gotten a lot of satisfaction out of our performances, both out at the bases, and all over. It had been a long road along the way, but well worth it and remembering what Steve whispered to me, we immediately went into Country Joe's "Gimme an F." The crowd went wild. They started singing along…

"One, Two, Three, what are we fightin' for…"
Shit, we had our own private "Woodstock" right there!

Rockin' Nam

I couldn't believe all the soldiers I saw. There were so many GIs ready for some rock n' roll ... to get their minds off their troubles. They all had pain, weather it was partying or going insane because a wife or girl friend was seeing someone else back home. They looked toward us for help, to get away from the "shit" for a while. I'm not sure if this is what Saigon had in mind when they began putting all these GI bands together, but it doesn't matter, we were there and we were doing what we were meant to do.

We finished the opening and everyone was settling into quite a groove. We were ragin' and they were ready. We immediately went into the second tune, "Have you ever seen the rain."

Guys were everywhere. They packed the grounds and hugged the stage. They couldn't get enough of us and the band and I were so honored.

We played some more songs and I finally started to see what we'd meant doing all year. I finally realized my worth and my role in this far-off distant place. I had recently become very introspective. I figured out that I wasn't sent there to type. And I wasn't sent there to pump gas. And I sure wasn't sent there to just PARTY! No, I was sent there to use my talent to contribute to the peace of mind and well-being of my fellow soldiers.

Those cool guys that didn't wanna be there but went anyway because they got orders and went to serve. I loved every one of them.

Rockin' Nam

I was honored to be in the position I was in. To be the one who, was part of a role to uplift the troops, was an honor. I began to cherish every day, especially after really seeing the picture much clearer. And when they showed appreciation, it was double.

We started in on our finale, "Closer to Home." It was a Grand Funk classic that we used all year to close the show. It became our "Mantra" and a kind of anthem. For many a soldier, everywhere, it was just the PERFECT song!

As we started that signature intro, I saw guys "tear up" when I started the first verse. By the time I got to the chorus many were so emotional, they had tears running down their faces. Some were "losin' it" as we kicked some ass. It's important to know that emotions were magnified here, some 10,000 miles away under these conditions.

We then played one of our most powerful songs—and so the finale began…

"Every – body, listen to me…and return me, my ship…I'm your Captain, I'm your Captain, though I'm feelin' mighty sick…"

I saw emotion in their faces. Guys were everywhere! Some, I remembered from earlier. Some I was in touch with around the places we had played. It was kind of eerie.

Rockin' Nam

I watched as they made their way to the front. I looked out to my right and—oh my God—there's Amy (the donut dolly, Red Cross worker), with a tear in her eye as she blew me a kiss. Wow! I could hardly maintain.

"I'm getting closer to my World."

We sang the refrain over and over as the crowd got more and more emotional and most were singing along. You talk about a key moment in an unbelievable year! This was definitely it! I don't think I'd trade any memory like this for anything. The song came to a close. We heard the familiar chant ... "MORE! MORE!"

We smiled at each other, shrugged our shoulders, and went into the Buddy Miles classic, "Them Changes." It was another one of our "can't miss" songs that worked every time. It had an infectious beat and awesome rhythm to it and any message that stated that GIs were going through "changes" was a real winner. It was very universal! Not quite sure what the GIs were hearing, but the band seemed to be feeling pretty good. We were on it. We played a nice long set. I looked out into the crowd and saw that Amy was really digging the music. She gave me an incredible smile. I thought I was going to melt

After these gigs, it was time to move on. I had got orders to go HOME! Everyone said the goodbyes, and we headed out. We all had grins on our faces and were truly "living the dream!" I felt a guilty because here I was, living the life of frolic.

Rockin' Nam

Deep down inside, I knew that soldiers, at times, were going through hell. I'm not saying I regretted the break to play music but every once in a while, the reality of guilt would smack me in the face. Still it was just something I was fated to do. At least, that's the way I saw it. Why else was I sent there? Just what was to be my role in the U.S. Army in VIETNAM? Hell, I didn't know how to *DO* anything else! The sun set on our show, the evening, and my year. A lot of people wanted to talk to us and take pictures afterward. Looking back, I wished I'd kept some of those pictures. They were classics and a record of a fantastic trip!

This gig was incredible evidence that encapsulated everything that was "us." And it was everything that we were supposed to be. The soldiers had come to really count on us and we were always trying to come through. On the surface it was just a "rockin" performance but if you dig a little deeper, it shows what they really needed. Imagine being out in the middle of nowhere day after day after day. So many guys were on the verge of getting to the end of their rope that I can't help but think we were in position to be somewhat of a help. In fact, I'm sure of it. The concert for sick GIs was interesting. It was a smart idea, set up to give guys a chance to take a break without having to leave the country. Some guys could only get away for this and the place was perfect for them. A lot of guys didn't know that we were coming but you should have seen the look on their faces when we finally hit the stage. It was a feeling like I've never known ... So we finished our big gig in front of the GIs, ABC, and everyone else. It was a trip and all very worth it. I still marvel today at some of the situations I ran into.

Questions still hang over my head. How in the world did I go to "Nam" and manage to get myself into this situation. The road to playing music, singing, and entertaining "USA-starved" soldiers was so worth it. They constantly thanked me for visiting them and I constantly told them I was just doing my job. I just kept reliving the very first moments I had arrived in this Southeast Asian paradise for the first time. *The chopper showed up* to pick me up and take me back and again, here comes all the dust. I climb in, and look who's on board — AMY! — on the Huey!

"What's going on, woman?" I asked.

"Long time, no see soldier; how's your tour going? I'll bet it's a wild ride."

"A wild ride, for sure — I didn't know all those guys were so sick, needing our help."

"Well you're the 'killer' band, they're put you to work." She complimented.

"Happy to do it," I said.

"Well, and that's why we love you." She smiles.

I was thinking how hard it was to be cool when she said things like that. I'd get chills ... melt inside. Again, we bobbed and weaved to Cam Ranh, and once again, I couldn't keep my eyes off of her. When we got there, she actually gave me a big hug.

"Maybe we'll even meet up back in the world,"

"Let's not push it, Private. I live in Colorado, and you?"

"California … but I could be on tour."

"Have a good trip," she smiled.

"Thanks, Ames," I said affectionately.

"God bless you, Rocker," she added.

"And the same to you," I said.

All I had were some pictures from earlier in the year. I often thought about how lucky I was to have *any pictures at all*—period! Throughout the year, after all the shows, we'd talk and tell endless stories of life on the road—the gigs, the girls, the drugs, the craziness …. The reflections of so many GIs were everywhere—every nook and cranny of Vietnam. There were so many wild stories. Everyone had a wild tale to tell.

There were a handful of GIs that were very comfortable where they were—like that guy we had met earlier. Why would they leave? They had lots of time; a steady, loving girl; and a nice constant stash of stuff. In fact, some of these guys had fulfilled their obligation and just never went home. Lots of families were in touch with Washington claiming POW or MIA and scared to death about what happened to their boy. Some may have been legitimately lost but it's a good bet there are still a handful over there and they're content.

Rockin' Nam

It's all up for debate and my intention isn't to demean or play this down. I know it's a serious subject that many people take to heart. I guess time will tell what happens.

Many soldiers at the concert were getting ready to go home. Of course, everyone exchanged numbers and vowed to get together "back in the world." Fact is, through the years there were very few get-togethers.

I saw three of my buds: Doug, Stoney, and Woody. I talked to two others on the phone—Chet and Booker. What a crack-up—guys like Sunshine, who had come over from the hills of Tennessee as a full-on, redneck hayseed, and within a month or so, turned into one of the biggest freaks in country.

There was Mac who came from Canada, but in time turned into US Army through and through. Stash and Gibo—these guys had the biggest mustaches around! As did most of these guys who served during the first half of my tour over there when things were loose... when we had all the freedom in the world. I didn't know how the other guys in country did it—the ones with the same routine day after day .... I'm not trying to dis' them, but for me, that would have driven me batty. In my world, things just seemed to be so wild and out of control ... and that's just the way I liked it. I got very used to it but in the end it would wind up being my undoing.

The next day I made my way back to Don Zume (for the last time). This time, I was really burnt. What was I going to do now? After all that's happened, I can't imagine doing anything else. After going through what I just went through—everything that went down— I think it would have been anticlimactic, to say the least.

I didn't have a lot of unfinished business to take care of, just the one habit, and now I was very SHORT (not much time left in-country). I wondered who'd be left at the 577th — *PROBABLY NOBODY!* I knew it'd be a shock to segue out of this and get mentally prepared for the "real" world. I had to start thinking in that direction.

As we trucked back to the home base, I started to reminisce again. I wondered where Amy was going to go. I wondered how Kim and Lin were doing. Did Woody make it back to San Diego? And the rest of my buds—are they going to be OK? Steve Bell? Is he still in-country? Did he go back to ABC? And all those kids at the POW camp? What about he Montegnard kids— what's their future? I tried not to put the weight of the world on my shoulders, but I often felt nostalgic and sad.

So now it's back to 577th. Don Zume, the place where we all sat out on the sandbagged rooftops at sunset and aired our feelings—good and bad—A place where every day at sundown the guys would gather at the water with their trucks and wash them down with pride to get them ready for their next dirty day.

Rockin' Nam

Don Duong, the place where "Big Jake" almost "gave up" until we used all our force and all of our energy to "love" him out of it. Yes, the 577th, a very special place for me and everyone else—a place where guys really *GREW* and matured and "came of age."This was the place where we felt the true nature of GI camaraderie and truly, a place like no other. I got to the base and wandered around for a few minutes. I knew no one! It was like a ghost town with spit shine.

I went to check in with the CO, but the new Cap was busy. I hung out in the office for a minute. I listened to some pretentious conversation between two office guys. There was just no place for me here! It couldn't have been weirder. Unbelievably, I sauntered down to the Ville. For some reason, no one stopped me.

I didn't go for drugs or women or anything. I just wanted to get away from the base … just wanted to wander. I made my way to an obscure end of town, and something wonderful happened. I heard music coming from a certain structure. I poked my nose in and to my amazement, it was a BAND! And they were PLAYING MUSIC!—AMERICAN MUSIC! I went in! As I got into the room, what a surprise—there they were … a teenage band rehearsing. A group of Vietnamese teens and they were working on a recognizable song! It was a tune called "Reflections of my life" by Marmalade.

"All my sorrows (all my sorrows) … here tomor—oh, oh, oh … take me back … to my home."

Rockin' Nam

I was very impressed, to say the least—really, I was! These young guys were passionately trying to make it happen! When you think about it, here they were in a war-torn area of the world with no money, no jobs, and trying to do the impossible—to play rock 'n' roll, and at sixteen and seventeen years old! They were jammin' out some American tune. I grabbed some juice and coffee and told them how much I liked them and wanted to maybe be their manager. They were thrilled.

I told them that I was on my way back to the highlands. I also told them I might be back. Before I left, I asked them what their hopes were for their band. They said that they wanted to get in the game—to improve on their sound. They wanted to grow like bands that came out of America and Europe. They were very cool, and I liked their style. I really wanted to help, but I was dreaming in reality. I was just acting on emotion from my nostalgic mood. They kind of reminded me of ME just a couple years back—young, eager, hyper—on a mission to further my musical aspirations. They were putting songs together and rehearsing, building hopes and dreams, trying to get to the top of the charts, like everybody else. I couldn't get over it! I ran into kids, in a band in the middle of nowhere, in 1971, in South Vietnam. They told me they could really use some equipment, some pedals, strings, maybe a wah-wah. I told them I'd try and do that for them, that I'd try and help them out, maybe be their manager. Maybe be their manager?— Sure…Here I am, a performer, at the ripe old age of nineteen and talking of managing a band ten thousand miles away.

This scene with the band could have been right out of the Lancaster film, *"Jim Thorpe–All-American."* After they stripped him of all those Olympic medals he won. He was so down that he wound up wandering aimlessly—anywhere and everywhere — taking jobs at circuses and carnivals. In the end, Thorpe walks through the projects near a dirt field with a bunch of kids playing football. The ball gets away from the kids and rolls over to him as he picks it up and sadly looks at it. In the film, the kid says,

"Hey mister, toss it over here. Throw it back … C'mon," they yelled.
"Mister! They insisted.
They kept yelling … it was dramatic.

Thorpe (Lancaster) then, picks it up and throws it a country mile. They smile at him as they all watch it soar over their heads. It was a healing experience, just the right thing at just the right time for me. A line in the film that really hit home was what the kids yell to him —
"Thanks, Coach! … way to go …."
"Coach?" I thought. "Was this my new role?"
I NEVER SAW THEM AGAIN

I got back, and the CO approached me.

"Son, you're going home. You've done your time here and a damn good job. I read up on you. Go to admin and pick up you orders!"

"HOLY SHIT!" I thought.

"My time was up and headed back to the world! Guess what just crept up on me?" I worried.

I didn't think the CO had the faintest idea who I really was or what I was all about, but I was glad he had a good impression of me. It gave me confidence. He just shook my hand, thanked me, and sent me on my way.

What a mind-f**k.

I puttered around for a couple days and gathered the few things I had left. I headed over to admin. I told them that I had lost my ID (again), and they printed me out a temporary. I was in a complete daze as I had gone full circle. I knew I had to keep it together through the debarkation process. Months ago, I was just landing as a naive, inexperienced cherry. At this moment, I now knew where those two freaks were coming from. It was a wild ride indeed. I prepared to go.

There was a dark cloud gathering over my head—might have been an omen. I caught a ride to Cam Ranh as I managed to "get outta dodge."

I probably wouldn't get another break. This time the urine test wouldn't be broken. I checked into the proper place, and I was very nervous. I recognized that, in the blink of an eye, I was no longer the big deal I once was, just a burnt-out GI. I was just another soldier trying to check out and go home. I had been very aware that this day would come. I thought about it constantly and tried to get prepared for it (half-heartedly) but it sure did just sneak up on me.

Not so sure I was ready for this, but here we go!

Ultimately I got ready to face the Grim Reaper ... I'd have to take that goddamned urine test but, so what? Everybody took it ... and they passed it! They were all partying!

I TOOK IT ... AND I FLUNKED IT!

I was shocked because I cut way down on partying. But, alas, I was officially a user. They told me I had to spend an extra week right there in Cam Ranh (behind a barbed-wire complex). I was also to spend an extra week at Fort Ord when I got back. They proceeded to put me in that "special" line. The night before the test, I wandered around the area.

This was the same place that just eleven months earlier, I first met all the guys, Big Dick, the freaks, Woody, Cap ... I was so freaked out that I tried to steal a big stereo from a guy (who I thought was sleeping). I almost got my ass beaten. The situation was this:

Some guy—a huge guy— started chasing me down for trying to steal his stereo. I had quietly tried to lift his boom box and tiptoed away. The big booming voice yells!

"HEY! What the HELL are you doing?"

Rockin' Nam

"WHERE YOU GOIN' WITH MY STEREO?"

"Uh, oh, BUSTED!" I had to think fast. Again, my wit and quickness emerged. I told him,

"I couldn't sleep ... I wanted to listen to some music."

The guy mellowed out a little and said,

"Well, you can listen. Just sit here — close by — and listen."

I was ashamed of myself. I remember thinking,

"This just may be the darkest part of my whole journey. I've had a lot of high-lights and a lot of lows but this is the worst, now it all comes crashing down. This was not going to be pretty."

I would now get ready to go through the most agonizing task of checking into an embarrassing, humiliating, ugly, barbed-wire concentration camp. This was so embarrassing; One day cheered at the concert of a lifetime and now sick, busted, and rehabbed. I felt so bad. What have I got myself into? Maybe, I should have tried a little harder to get out of this final piss test.

After all, I *DID* have some celebrity, some "pull" and a lot of connections. You would have thought I could have tried for some favors, but I guess I didn't have it together enough to play politics. It seems like I was just another GI busted! I was exhausted as I got to the complex. It was dark and scary. The place reeked of disappointment and failure. I tried to think of happier times — those first couple days in Cam Ranh, the freaks,

Big Dick, Cap—all of it. Most guys were busy trying to concentrate on putting the year into prospective, keeping their noses clean, and getting their asses back home. I was trying to keep my shit straight, and I was in that "close-my-eyes-and-get-it-over-with" mode.

I tried to stay positive, although it was tough. If I could just get through this week and then get back home to begin my life again, I'd be alright—to wipe the slate clean and start all over. That famous adage kept going through my head...

"Hey ... you play, you pay!"

HOMEWARD BOUND
11.

They inspected us—all of us—and I mean every part of us. They wanted to make sure that we weren't carrying in anything we weren't supposed to have—anywhere. They checked every orifice on our persons and told us how it "was gonna be!" Apparently, we were to spend several days there at "Camp DRYOUT" while the drugs washed out of our system.

I didn't have a good feeling about this. How ugly was it going to get? How in the FUCK did I get myself into this situation? I should have been smarter. What's going to happen now? The group also included several Black Militants who were constantly chanting, "You're gonna die with your people."

"SHIT! Black militants … coming down off smack; are you kidding me?"

A couple hours later, they led us to the complex which was hidden away in a remote area of Cam Ranh. I went into a Quonset hut full of cots lined up on both sides. I was thoroughly down and depressed. Everything had finally caught up with me. I had reached rock bottom, and I knew it. I laid down on a bed and fell fast asleep. I was thrashed. I thought I'd seen it all and done it all in my time in "the Nam," but *THIS* really made me stop and think. It was pretty sad. I awoke in the darkness. I felt like shit. No one was there.

Rockin' Nam

At first, I didn't know where I was. I'd been dreaming, and I couldn't decipher between fantasy and reality for a minute. I was out of it. After a few minutes, it started to sink in. I got busted! I got high — now I don't have any more stuff. I dragged my ass up and tried to figure it out. I heard voices outside. I slowly made my way to the door. I opened the door and there they were — all the rehabs, sitting in chairs on the sand. They were sitting on the wall, on the ground, or wherever they could find a seat. They were all smoking their Kools and Marlboros, drinking Fresca. They looked like shit.

There was a Donut Dolly there. Her name was Emily. (I would come to find out later that Emily was one of the most popular dollies in all of Vietnam). She was sitting in a beach chair near a faded sandstone wall. She was nice, and she was cute — but she wasn't Amy. I asked her if she knew Amy. She didn't. Anyway, Emily was sitting in front of a card table with some cookies and punch. There was also a little guitar standing upright and leaning against the hut.

"What time is it?" I asked gruffly.

"Nine," she replied.

"Morning or night?" I winced, (big laughs).

"What? But I'm hungry," I growled.

"I'm sorry Pfc."

(I was a private first class; I made it to E-4, but they busted me for the 'Cali'-jacket' fiasco).

"You missed chow, but you're welcome to some cookies and punch."

"Jesus," I sighed. One guy yells…

"He can't help you now," (more laughter).

I walked over and grabbed a handful of cookies. I chugged a cup of punch. I asked if I could see her guitar.

"Oh, you play?" she said.

"A little," I sheepishly boasted.

A few had recognized me from the gigs. I picked up the guitar, and I could hear a couple guys whisper from a distance,

"Watch this!"

I picked it up and started riffing. The guys got silent. Emily was impressed. I kept at it ... getting into a groove. Some of the guys were amazed. Some of the guys started speaking up—

"Hey, you're that guy from that band," one of them said.

"Yeah, that show last week ... near Saigon," said another.

Another one, "Yeah, I saw you in Pleiku."

I tried to hush them both up, but the word spread around the sand. I was happy to get the accolades but totally embarrassed to be in this position. The dolly was suddenly very impressed. She was now treating me totally differently than when I walked out there. We all partied for an hour or so, and then Emily said,

"OK, this was fun, but now it's that time to go."

A collective groan rang out. Slowly, and one by one, they retreated to the inside of the Quonset hut. Everyone was hurting, deliberately and slowly walking to bed. I was spaced.

I began milling around my bunk when (like Doug, months ago), I thought I heard something. I DID! "Psssst."

I looked across the aisle.

Rockin' Nam

I saw this kind of light-skinned, Black dude with a huge 'fro. I nodded to him and he beckoned for me to come over. He proceeded to introduced himself to me. He turned to be pretty cool. We hit it off pretty good.

"Hey, I'm Ron from San Jose … mom's White, dad's Black." He went on —

"What the hell are you doing here?"

"How did you wind up in this place? You're awesome!" I tried to be humble.

"Well, I was doing pretty well until I had to leave country. I partied hard and got caught in the end, didn't I? Like everyone here, I just couldn't stop."

I shook his hand and gave him a little dap (brother hand shake routine). He couldn't get over the fact that I was in there. He couldn't stop complimenting me.

"You're amazing! Can't believe you're here?"

"Well, I started playing when I was a kid, came into the Army, got orders over here, and I just finished rocking for a year … now I'm here," I explained.

"LIGHTS OUT!" Emily yells.

The lights went out, but we continued to talk and we kept talking. We had a lot in common.

He thought I was so good that he gave me a pick.

"Here, I got this from a backstage friend at the Filmore…it's yours now."

He handed me a pick with Jimi Hendrix's signature on it. The time at rehab actually went by pretty quick. I was aching but we *DID* manage to straighten out (for the most part) and reflected on all our memories. When it came time to leave, they paraded everyone out to a C-130 in our pajamas.

Rockin' Nam

We all packed into the plane which was gutted out except for a hundred or more seats. On the way over to 'Nam, everyone *LOST* a day. Now, on the way home, we would *GAIN* one back. To tell you the truth, I didn't know WHAT day it was — not to mention — what month or what year. I felt like Roy Scheider's character in *Jaws*, when at the end of the movie, he asked ...

"What day is it?"

All I knew is that we were going home (with an overnight stop in Yokota, Japan). Couple hours into the flight, a few more guys recognized me — AND IN MY PJs! They started complimenting me, over and over. They all wanted to hear some more music. One of the guys found a small guitar in the baggage and approached me.

"We need some music; can you play us one?

"I can't." I mumbled selfishly.

"C"mon," another pleaded.

Now they were all bummed. They insisted, and I felt for them. I always felt for them. I was feeling nostalgic and said, "OK, OK."

I remembered that I was never one to turn a soldier down. They all got quiet. I took the guitar and made sure it was fairly in tune, and then I started playing "Tequila." (Even though there's no singing and wasn't a saxophone around for miles).

"Just kidding," I jested.

The guys chuckled a little but were still adamant about the song. I thought long and hard as I tinkered. I played around on the strings a little bit and looked up. I saw all the faces with "need" in their eyes, even more than before. My heart was heavy.

Rockin' Nam

I became very introspective as I went into a somber acoustic intro. While I played, I was thinking...

"How'd these guys spot me? How'd they find me a guitar? What a great bunch of guys these are ... Oh well, no matter where I went, seems like they'd forever find me. One thing, we all have to have music, that's for sure!"

I continued to do an improvised acoustic collage of triads and ad-libbed some modal riffs that no one recognized. As I improvised, I was thinking of just how I could get out of this. It wasn't that I didn't like the guys, it was more like, "How embarrassing ... I wish I wasn't here."

I piddled some more until I rested on the "C" chord. Then I hit them with—

"I'm sittin' in the railway station, got a ticket for my destina-shuun ... on a tour of one-night stands, my suitcase and guitar in hand ..."

That's right, the hard-hitting, soulful rendition of Paul Simon's "Homeward Bound," a song I learned growing up when it first came out—a very cool acoustic ballad. I remember this song so well.

It had an incredible sentimentality to it and was so masterfully composed by Simon from the album, *"Parsley, Sage, Rosemary, and Thyme."* I stopped and tuned up.

I looked around the dark, dingy inside fuselage. I got to the chorus and guys started singing along. I was very moving. Seems I've been through this movie before. It was Deja Vu. These guys were so emotional at this point. The fact was that we were going home!

The scene was gripping ... more than a hundred GIs (in their pajamas), tears in their eyes! Singing! ... All participating in the familiar lament—

> *"HOME, WHERE MY THOUGHTS ESCAPING*
> *HOME, WHERE THE MUSIC'S PLAYING*
> *WHERE MY LOVE LIES WAITING*
> *SILENTLY FOR ME."*

... another unforgettable moment!

We eventually landed in Yokota, Japan and everyone was thrilled. Get this! There were actual beds! And TVs!—with no more cigarette commercials! And candy machines! We hadn't seen a candy bar in a year. Even though it was just another military base, it was way better that what we'd had for the past year.

We spent a couple days in Japan, before we shipped to Fort Ord. In California I was happy in a way but totally depressed. I was detoxing from all the craziness one could pack into a one-year period. It was around this time that I made another mistake—I called home. My mother was thrilled to hear from her son, so was everyone else back home. After all, I made them proud when I came home right in the middle of basic training for a Christmas break. So impressive; I was in my new army uniform.

But can you imagine how euphoric they were to hear that I was back from 'Nam?

"Sorry," was the only thing I could say. I needed some space and I needed some time to mellow out.

My dad had a cool attitude—

"OK, then, I guess we'll see ya when we see ya."

Rockin' Nam

I tried to shrug it off after I hung up but it weighed on my mind. After all, this thing started when I ran away from home in June of '69. So, in actuality, it appeared that this had been a three-year ordeal.

I thought (sarcastically) But hey, we're going home! *It's all over now, but the paperwork.*

One thing I WAS thinking right around this time—"How was the army going to release us? What category would we be put in?"

The answer finally came. They let us "rehabbers" off easy. Everyone got out of their pajamas and into their fatigues.

DIG THIS: We all got—*HONORABLE DISCHARGES!*

EPILOGUE

How, in the world, I got an honorable is way beyond me. What a break! I said goodbye to everyone and walked on down the road. As soon as I got to the bus station, I took my duffle bag, went into the bathroom, and put my jeans on. I finally started feeling like a civilian again.

As I walked out, can you believe it?—Ten Years Afters', "Goin' Home" was playing through the shitty bus station speakers! No Shit! I was now a civilian again. Hard to believe, but I had just went through one of the biggest "mind-fucks" of all time.

To my friends and family's amazement, the "discharge papers" really blew them away. There were no asterisks or additions—just honorable! This would forever signify that I did my time although deep down inside, I knew I was lucky. I screwed around way too much, and wound up always getting in trouble. It could have been way worse. The only saving grace for me was the hours I entertained the soldiers and made their lives better.

When we got out on the street, I checked out pretty quickly. I got to the bus station, went in and changed into jeans and a sweatshirt. As I rode the Trailways down the coast, I was still reeling. I'd just been to "bizarre and back," and it was all starting to sink in.

Rockin' Nam

I stared out the window as scenes from the entire year played back right in front of me in the reflection of the windows. I couldn't think about some of the memories or I'd start crying in public.

I swear, as the bus pulled out onto the highway and down the 101, a GI a few rows further up on the bus aisle turned up his stereo and Zepplin's, "Goin' to California" played at full volume...perfect! Now, I definitely had to regroup, get back to where I was, and where I wanted to be—but where *WAS* I really?

I wanted to take this whole valuable experience (crammed into one year) and move forward. I thought about it as I looked out at the countryside along the 101 and lay my head back. I was thinking that California was pretty much just as I remembered it. I couldn't wait to get back and see everyone and to play some music, and decide what my next venture was going to be.

I have told this story for years, and vowed one day to get it done – To write it. Now, I've done it...So many people to thank in the last forty-some years that helped me make it happen.

Many celebrities, industry people, and all-around creative people I met up with along the way also marveled at the unique story, and their sentiments were all the same. People like Nick Nolte, Liz Montgomery, and others.

Jason Robards loved the idea. They all had similar reactions and made comments such as, "Let me know what happens with that" or "Sounds great .... Great story!" and the ultimate, "It would make a great film!"

In January of '14, I mentioned it to Robin Williams one night in Marin County. I showed him the book. He loved it. He told me to "go for it."

There were so many people that complimented me. Some saw the book on Amazon and smiled. Some gave me rave reviews. I appreciate that. As some people know, I never worked so hard on a project. She even loved the book but... Oh well...what might have been.

I wanted to see everybody and tell them about my year. However, I must not have been too homesick because just two weeks after I got back, Dana and I got out of town. We hitchhiked to Fort Collins, Colorado— IN THE WINTER! I believe we went up Highway 99 to 80 East through Reno and eventually Salt Lake. I distinctly remember being silly and jamming vocal licks to "Suite: Judy Blue Eyes" in the middle of the Wasatch mountains. The natural echo was amazing. It was fun to sing our hearts out in the middle of nowhere.

The next day, as we were singing in the mountains once again and a country girl stopped to pick us up. She wasn't going that far, but we took the ride nevertheless. My friend sat in the back, and I rode shotgun. It was a beautiful drive through the snow-draped mountains. The sun was beaming light down on the beautiful terrain. In no time, she was asking if I would drive for a while ... so she could maybe relax?

"Sure, I can do that," I said.

"Great!" she exclaimed.

Trying not to crack up, I saw my friend roll his eyes in the back seat. It was starting to become obvious that she had a bit of an interest in me. That was even more obvious when she put her hand on my knee and started rubbing my jeans. By this time, my friend had conked out. She smiled at me and, with her index finger, began to gently rub. In a matter of minutes, she knew she had me. She spoke up—

"We're almost to my place ... do you think you might want to come in for a while?"

I told her that I'd love to, but my friend was with me and that we should really move on.

My buddy woke up as she dumped our asses out near the Wyoming border.

It didn't take long for us to get busted by the state police in Wyoming for hitchhiking; what? What kind of bullshit is this! We cooperated completely but in private, I couldn't stop bitching about it. The guy even gave us a ride. We got to the bus station, and wired home for some money to buy two tickets to Fort Collins—trippy! When we got to CSU, we headed straight for the quad. When we got there, we went right for the campus radio station. I'll never forget seeing the front of the university for the first time. As we came down the walkway, we saw the tree-lined sidewalk where the grass and trees were adorned with snow. This "postcard" continued straight down the sidewalk of the 200-year-old campus.

... (*Don't forget. This is the same university where Jimmy Stewart's character sat and proposed to June Allyson character while filming, "The Glenn Miller Story."*)

I decided to call my Nam buddies. I rang Doug. He lived in Mansura, Louisiana, and he couldn't believe that he was hearing from me. He told me that Stoney was around, and that we should come on down.

He wanted to hook up as promised back in Saigon. The band was so good back then and we both had dreams of making it again.

"I'd like to Doug, but we're broke, I said. "The cops made us buy bus tickets in Wyoming because it was illegal to hitchhike there."

I explained that we had made it to Fort Collins, Colorado, and that we were strapped for cash.

"It took all we had to just GET here!" I said.

"OK, we'll just have to come up and get you," Doug answers.

"WHAT? No way—REALLY?" I said, smiling big and wide.

We wound up in the great state of Louisiana. Just as years prior as I got into the army in the first place, playing music in *LOUISIANA*? (Looks like I've come full circle). When we got there, we all hooked up with Stoney. It was wonderful. We were in seventh heaven. It was just like we planned it. Later, we went on as a trio because my buddy had to return to "Cali" and so the three of us toured Texas and Louisiana from place to place. We went on to play New Orleans, Houston, Austin, and places in-between.

We picked up right where we left off from Saigon. We were as wild as ever but, fortunately, none of us were looking for powder.

SIDENOTE: The three of us—all "Vietnam vets"—came home, formed a band, and collected all our benefits at the same time ... unemployment medical, and other benefits. We'd gotten together, jammed, carried on, and had a ball doing all the gigs. Years later, I would tell my good friend, Richie, that sadly, while I did my two years in the service, Janis died ... Jimi died ... Jim Morrison passed, and just for good measure, the VERY day I got home—THE VERY DAY!—Duane Allman was killed (on his birthday) riding his motorcycle. It was an era right in the middle of the "Woodstock" generation ... I came home, just grabbed my guitar and walked on. I thought about all the gigs we did entertaining the troops ... and I've never stopped. A year of "giggin' with the heavies!" ...Truly one of a kind!

Lots of people to thank relating to this venture.

To my dear friend and sax guy, SCOTT PAGE, who's has been pushing me to write this book for years. Scott is an incredible talent. I'll remember him constantly nagging me, "FLYN, YOU GOTTA WRITE IT!" He wasn't the only one who said that...others expressed the same but Scott really hammered it home.

To all my brothers and sisters, friends and family... to all I have told this story and vowed one day to get it done. There are so many people in the last several years ... good friends like Allan and Elsie who would often sit and listen with fervor—it felt good. Everyone really thought I had a unique and original story.

To our ABC correspondent, Steve Bell, who heard about, took an interest, and filmed us. Big thanks. You were so cool and supportive and made us feel important and relevant in the big picture—thank you! It's been a roller-coaster ride for sure. All the people I've met, all the places I passed through—I'm eternally grateful.

Big thanks to my family and friends. Huge thanks to my mom and dad, to my sister, Martha, and her family, and to all the Flynns. They've been very generous.

Also, to my friends and musicians like the drummer, Chet, who also shot some of the pictures in the book ... and to my friend and bass player, Chicano (wherever you are). He shot a lot of the pics as well. Also, to all the Grosswendt's especially, "Big Mike."

I *would like to give it up to* the 577th Engineer Battalion in Don Duong. They were so awesome.

To the 35th Engineer Battalion in Cam Ranh ... the *Stars and Stripes* newspaper ... whoever was playing that GREAT music at all the bases on AFVN radio. To my CO at the 577th, to Captain Jack at Cam Ranh, to all my army buds, to all those wonderful "Donut Dollies", to my band members, and everyone that contributed to my crazy trip—I'm forever grateful.

Big kudos to all the musicians that spent time in 'Nam, and to the people I've told this story to through the years who gave me the encouragement to keep it in mind, to pursue this project, and go public with it.

Enormous thanks to my dear friend, David Brooke, who gave me a place to stay and the tools and information to publish this book—thanks, Babe! To Rick and Case who also gave me housing, friendship, and feedback. Also, to my cousins, Lisa and Karl—thank you! And to my cousin, Maureen, you're the best! Big shout out to Tom and Renee, my good friend, Eric Streit, the Siegels. Many thanks to Marisa Everett, Kathy, Lori, for the help! I hope I have made everyone proud.

Rockin' Nam

To my uncle Bob, who changed my life! You took me in, brought me into Hollywood, hooked me up with a songwriting gig at eighteen, and got going!

Finally, I'd like to thank God … for giving me the strength, spirit, determination, to have this experience and make it through. It was a tough job, but I finally but I finally was able to recall most everything and pen this book. Thank the Lord for keeping my memory intact, for keeping me alert and for bringing me back safe so I could reflect back and write this story.

… and the beat goes on!

PROPS

DONUT DOLLY.COM

WAR STORIES.COM

WOMEN OF HISTORY

PERSONAL PICS – '70-'71

NATURAL ACHIVES

CHET ELLINGSON PICS

HOMEBOY SNAPSHOTS

MIKE GROSSWENDT PHOTOS

GINNY, TOM & RENEE

JIM & JANA, GREGG– KENNY O.

DARA – D.C. – BUDDY

EARLE, DICK & BOB T.

LORI, MARISA, SCOTT PAGE

ALL FLYNNS & GROSSWENDTS

TO SMACKEY – ELLEN

AND TO ERIC STREIT

The News!

ABC's Steve Bell, one of the hippest newsmen around. He filmed the band inside the officers' club during a big show at China Beach in Da Nang.

Tuning up for the road ... truck is packed with guitars, amps, and M-16s.

The INFAMOUS "CALI" JACKET ... They took pictures and sent them on to the authorities because I was apparently committing fashion crimes!

This picture of me out of uniform and flipping the bird to authorities landed me in "BUKU" trouble.

Chet … great drummer and all-around nice guy … we sure rode that roller coaster together and had a wild time in the 'Nam.

MR. SMOOTH, Charles Booker …our bass player … played with Curtis Mayfield and others before arriving in 'Nam … he had a great style and definitely helped made the band sound great!

Rockin' Nam

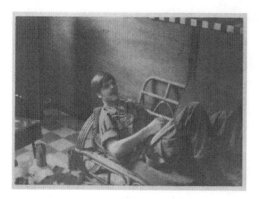

Doug … bassist, vocals, and equipment tech…This story doesn't happened if it weren't for him! Always loved dropping in on him... He was my "rock."

Stoney (Preston) … classically-trained keyboardist … we had fun jamming in Saigon and all around 'Nam. We would later hook up in Baton Rouge, Houston, and Austin after our return in '72.

Rockin' Nam

Gary was from
Payson, Arizona
so we called him
"ARIZONA" ...
very talented
musician ...

"Stash" (from San Francisco) ... We had
too much fun in the Central Highlands
... and also got into our share of trouble.

Emily was another very popular Donut Dolly. We met at the rehab compound before I was allowed to leave country.

Gibo ... He and I had some crazy days in 1971 ... taking kids for ice cream to Dalat and lots of other adventures...

I never had second thoughts about going into
the service ... after all, even Jimi went in!

Hendrix fan...in "Nam" and back in the world!

Lin... worked at CMTS (Command Military Touring Shows). They were headquartered in Saigon.

15 year-old roadie, "Boy-san "

Crazy good!

A common scene at various spots
around the country ... sadly it never really
got better until years later....

Although never really a fan, he gave us a letter of accommodation nevertheless...

Hard to believe...

Traci and I at a book signing

Rockin' Nam

"The beginning" — 1970

"The end" – 1971 – we would become one of the most popular bands in the land … the "Woodstock-like" concert near Saigon was the perfect ending….

It was like "Woodstock!"

Cam Rahn lighter - 1971

Steve Bell ... modern day

Garage band - 1966

Dana, Richie, Ott, and me — 1999

The check-in "snack shack"
at Cam Ranh

Fly like an Eagle

Special Accommodation from General Abrams (through General Westmoreland)… for our musical contributions in 1971 … Thanks for the memories!

1971

ABOUT THE AUTHOR

Huck Flyn is a writer, singer, blues guitarist, comic, and California resident. He started playing music at age eleven, did his first gig at twelve, wrote his first song at thirteen, and went into the studio at fourteen. Now, he's played several major clubs and venues all over the country.

Huck is about to celebrate fifty years in the business. He has played clubs, amphitheaters, colleges, and places everywhere, including the world-famous Troubadour. In addition, he's played the Lesher, the Coach House, and the Riviera Hotel—just to name a few. Huck has opened for Joe Walsh, Marshall Tucker, Eddie Money, Nicolette Larson, Elvin Bishop, Kathy Mattea, Starship, CCR, Travis Tritt, Sha Na Na, and many others. He's also toured with several acts out of LA, Vegas, and elsewhere. Huck has done several benefits for causes such as twelve-step programs in the Midwest, and performances for Tony La Russa's ARF (Animal Rescue Foundation), in the Bay area.

Rockin' Nam

He was a featured actor and a key songwriter on the musical score of Kenny Ortega's genius rock musical, *"Bimbo's Cosmic Circus"* (performed at the Starwood in Hollywood in 1974 and San Diego in 1975).

Huck also toured with actor, Dwayne Jessie who, in 1985, was reprising his *Animal House* role as Otis Day on the college circuit in the East and thanks to his good friend, Sal, he and his band appeared on *Knots Landing* in 1987 (which replayed as the most popular "Knots" in 1989). Finally, at age eighteen (in 1969), thanks to his uncle Bob, he went to work as a young songwriter for Marshal Leib at Frankie Laine's publishing company in Hollywood. Soon after, he left for New Orleans to tour with a pop band.

After "The Big Easy," he entered the US Army in November 1969. He eventually got orders to Vietnam where he lied, schemed, and finagled his way into a rock band and went on "the tour that would never end!" Only eight days in-country, he was out entertaining his fellow GIs. He spent his entire year in "the Nam" making music. The band would play some of the hippest music of the time. His year in Vietnam was one of the craziest times anyone could imagine, and the author captured it all here in his own words.

Today, Huck lives between Ventura County, the Bay area, and Seattle. He spends lots of time in the studio, on the road, as well as writing and recording. He is working on the film, *Rockin' Nam,* and a new blues record. He also tours veterans' groups, military bases, clubs and facilities all over the country, doing shows, playing music, shaking hands, and doing book signings.

Rockin' Nam

The author donates portions of his entertainment
earnings to the following charities:

MUSICIANS ON A MISSION CALIFORNIA

WOUNDED WARRIOR PROJECT

GARY SINESE FOUNDATION

Huck is an Anaheim Ducks fanatic…

A Boise State rooter

&

A Notre Dame Football fan.

Rockin' Nam

Huck Flyn has worked with :

Albert King – Albert Collins – Elvin Bishop –
Pat Travers – Loudon Wainwright III -
Sha Na Na – Joe Walsh – Johnny Rivers –
Max Karl & Glenn Frey – Nicolette Larson
David Benoit - Redbone- Richard Elliott
.38 Special - Huey Lewis -America- Otis Day
The Marshall Tucker band - Rosemary Butler
– New Grass Revival-Kathy Mattea-Tokens
Three Dog Night-The Tubes – BTO - Kansas
Commander Cody – David Lindley-Kenny O.
Cheap Trick – Chris Montez – Tim Goodman
George Thorogood-Ambrosia-Joey Scarbury
Teresa James – Paul Williams - Al Stewart -
Black Oak Arkansas–Travis Tritt – and more

ROCKIN' NAM

HUCK FLYN

"ROCKIN' NAM"

© 2018 FLYNSTONE BOOKS & BEYOND

www.huckflyn.net

Rockin' Nam

1969

2009

Rockin' Nam

DEDICATED TO:

ALL BRAVE AMERICANS,

EVERYWHERE, WHO SERVE

SO WE CAN LIVE FREE.

Rockin' Nam

Rockin' Nam

And mercifully, it ends

Rockin' Nam

Rockin' Nam

Rockin' Nam

ROCKIN' NAM

© 2018

flynstone books & beyond

www.huckflyn.net

Proof

Made in the USA
Columbia, SC
07 February 2018